Eighth Edition

Family Financial Management

Instructions & Forms

SOUTH-WESTERN
CENGAGE Learning™

Australia • Brazil • Japan • Korea • Mexico • Singapore • Spain • United Kingdom • United States

SOUTH-WESTERN
CENGAGE Learning™

Family Financial Management, Eighth Edition

Vice President of Editorial, Business:
Jack W. Calhoun

Vice President/Editor-in-Chief:
Karen Schmohe

Acquisitions Editor: Eve Lewis

Sr. Developmental Editor: Dr. Inell Bolls

Marketing Manager: Michael Cloran

Marketing Coordinator: Linda Kuper

Content Project Manager: Corey Geissler

Manager of Technology: Mike Jackson

Manufacturing Coordinator: Kevin Kluck

Production Service:
International Typesetting and Compositon

Senior Art Director: Tippy McIntosh

Internal Designer: Lou Ann Thesing

Cover Designer: Lou Ann Thesing

Cover Images: ©Getty Images, Image Source; ©Fotosearch, Comstock; ©Getty Images, Trinette Reed, Digital Vision

Library of Congress Control Number: 2008037767

ISBN-13: 978-0-538-44862-8

ISBN-10: 0-538-44862-8

South-Western
5191 Natorp Boulevard
Mason, OH 45040
USA

For your course and learning solutions, visit **www.school.cengage.com**

Printed by RR Donnelley, U.S.A.
3 4 5 6 7 12

Contents

Part 1 Getting Started

Performance Outcomes

In Part 1 of this simulation, you will learn to:

1. Recognize key terms.
2. Identify all the components of this simulation.
3. Organize all the components in the file folder.
4. Describe the general purpose of this simulation.

Talking About Money

"Wow, your parents' house is lovely," said Celina as she sat relaxing on the deck. "The deck is great and the backyard is so big."

"Yeah, my brother and I loved growing up here," replied Tyra. "We spent lots of time playing in this yard."

"This is a perfect yard for children and for entertaining family," said Celina. "Jared and I have been talking about starting to save for a down payment on a bigger house with a nice yard."

"Saving!" Tyra laughed. "That's tough. I can't even save enough money for a new couch."

Tyra was visiting her parents, Lydia and Gary Burns. Her parents were enjoying the last days of summer by hosting a backyard cookout. They had invited Tyra and several friends and neighbors, including Jared and Celina Hoffman, who live around the corner.

Lydia walked up just in time to hear Tyra mention a new couch. "Tyra," said her mother, "I thought you were planning to buy a new couch months ago."

"I was," she replied, "but I just never seem to have enough money. It's like I'm not in control of my spending."

"I remember being the same way when I was your age," said Jared as he joined the group on the deck. "I had enough money for rent and stuff, but I could never scrape together enough money for big purchases. Celina helped me start paying attention to our money."

"Yes, Jared," Celina chuckled. "I seem to recall that you had a little trouble living within our budget at first."

Jared laughed and hugged his wife. "You're right, I did. But I got used to it. Come to think of it, Tyra, have you ever tried to make a budget for yourself?"

"No, not really. I'm not even sure what a budget is."

"It's simple," said Celina. "A budget is a plan for your money—so you'll know where it's going. If you want, we can get together sometime and I'll show you how to make a budget."

"Thanks, Celina," said Tyra with a smile. "I think I could use the help."

Looking Ahead

Everyone, regardless of age, has to deal with money. We all have to plan how we're going to earn money and what we're going to do with it when we get it. It doesn't matter how much money you earn, or how old you are, or if you're single or married, you still have to think about your money, or your **finances**. And everyone has to form a plan, or **budget**, for how to spend and save money. A budget will help you plan for necessary expenses and use the rest of your income to buy or save for the things you want most.

FYI *Watch for key terms as you read. These terms and their definitions appear in the glossary.*

In this simulation, you're going to take a look at the financial circumstances of several people: a young single person, a single father with one child, and a married couple in their thirties who don't have any children. In each of the three situations, you'll go through one month's worth of money-related events to see how these people keep track of their money and how they make decisions about their finances. Although their lives, incomes, and goals are very different, you'll discover how they all share a need to plan for their money.

We'll begin each part by introducing you to the characters in more detail. You will see how they figure out their **net worth** (how much they own minus how much they owe) and create their budgets. Then, day-by-day, we'll show you what happens to their finances—when paychecks come in and when they pay bills and make purchases. You are responsible for helping the characters keep track of the money coming in and going out. And every once in a while, we'll ask you a few questions to help you think about why these events and decisions are so important.

CHECKPOINT

How is *budget* defined in the glossary?

Getting Organized

To help you keep track of all the financial activities, we've provided several important items in this simulation:

- A *Financial Record Book* where you will write down all the money received and spent over the course of the month. (Some students may receive a data CD for this purpose.)
- A checkbook to practice writing checks. The checkbook includes a **checkbook register** that you will use to record deposits, written checks, and electronic transactions.

- A *Forms and Documents* section at the back of this instruction book. This section contains all the forms, receipts, and other documents related to the characters.
- A file folder with tabbed dividers for organizing all of the used forms and documents.

Locate each of these items. Tell your teacher if any item is missing. Place the tabbed dividers in alphabetical order in the simulation file folder: Checks Written, Deposits, Forms, Receipts. As you complete the transactions, file the documents behind the proper tab in the file folder. When you finish work each day, store this instruction book in the file folder, in front of the four tabs.

Are you ready to learn more about money, finances, and budgeting? Let's begin with Tyra, a young, single woman who's just learning about financial planning.

CHECKPOINT

What is a checkbook register used for?

Jump$tart Coalition for Personal Financial Literacy

National Standards in K-12 Personal Finance Education

Planning and Money Management

Standard 2: *Develop a system for keeping and using financial records.*

There is no one perfect system for keeping financial records. People need to develop systems that meet their specific needs. Although there are many products available for organizing records, you don't need anything fancy to do a good job of keeping track of things.

Activities

1. Describe your current system for keeping financial records. How might the system change in the next few years?
2. Ask several family members or adult acquaintances to explain the system they use for keeping financial records. Make a table comparing the two systems. Highlight the similarities and differences.

Special Topics

Locate the following Special Topic readings on the Data CD. Read the article and answer the Think It Through questions that appear at the end of the article.

- Special Topic 1: A Time and Place for Everything
- Special Topic 2: Know Your Limit
- Special Topic 3: Your Personal Financial Plan

Part 2 On Your Own

Performance Outcomes

In Part 2 of this simulation, you will learn to:

1. Determine a single person's net worth.
2. Plan a realistic budget for a single person.
3. Record a person's daily financial activities in a record book or in a computer file.
4. Organize the receipts, forms, and other paperwork involved in financial activities.
5. Maintain a checking account, including making deposits, writing checks, and balancing a checkbook register.
6. Use an automated teller machine (ATM) and a debit card.
7. Make smart purchasing decisions that fit within a person's budget.
8. Evaluate a person's financial activities at the end of each month.

Meet Tyra M. Burns

© Getty Images, Image Source

Tyra M. Burns is 24 years old. She lives alone in her own apartment at 4500 Red Maple Lane, Apartment 115, Maplewood, Ohio 44920. It is a small, one-bedroom apartment in an older building that doesn't have any extras like a pool or gym. Tyra pays $450.00 a month to live there. The rent includes the cost of some **utilities**, or essential services. The utilities included in her rent are water and trash collection, but not gas and electricity. She pays for gas and electricity and for phone service separately. Her phone number is (419) 555-2010. Her Social Security number is 333-22-8888. Tyra owns a used car that her parents bought for her a few years ago. Every month, she gives them a check for $200.00 to pay them back.

Three years ago, Tyra graduated from the local community college with an associate's degree in business management. Now she works full time as the assistant manager of the Water Point Grille, a family-style restaurant. She receives one paycheck on the first of every month. Tyra's boss is training her to become the manager in a few months. Someday, Tyra would like to own her own restaurant, maybe a fast-food **franchise**. When Tyra is not working, she likes to hang out with her friends, usually playing basketball or watching sports on TV.

Tyra earns $32,400 a year, and she tries to be careful with her money. She doesn't have any credit cards, so she writes checks to pay for bills and larger expenses. Lately, she hasn't been happy with the way she has been spending and the fact that she can't seem to save any money for expensive things, like a vacation or furniture. Maybe her friend Celina can help her take control of her money by showing her how to plan a budget.

CHECKPOINT

How much does Tyra earn each month?

Figuring Out Tyra's Net Worth

Shortly after the backyard cookout, Tyra and Celina sat down to take a look at Tyra's finances. Celina explained that Tyra should first figure out her net worth, so she would know how much money she really has.

Gathering Information

Tyra made a list of her **assets**, or the cash and other items she owns that are worth money:

- $740.12 in a checking account
- $69.65 in a savings account
- A savings bond worth $200.00 given to her by her grandmother
- Current value of her used car, $3,700.00
- Value of her personal items, $1,200.00
- $90.00 in cash

Then she made a list of her **liabilities**, or the money she owes:

- $1,400.00 to her parents for her car
- October rent, $450.00
- Tri-County Gas & Electric bill, $42.53
- Maplewood Telephone Company bill, $35.95

Filling Out Tyra's Net Worth Form

Celina and Tyra used a form to figure out Tyra's net worth. You can find the answer for yourself. Remove Form 1, page 53 of the *Forms and Documents* section of this instruction book, or access NETWORTH on your Data CD. Complete the form using the amounts shown above.

1. Write Tyra M. Burns on the blank line at the top.
2. Complete the assets section.
   a. List the amount of each asset in the proper space on the left-hand side of the form.
   b. Add the amounts and write the total amount on the correct line.
3. Complete the liabilities section.
   a. List the amount of each liability on the right-hand side of the form.
   b. Add the amounts and write the total amount on the correct line.
4. Determine Tyra's net worth by subtracting the total liabilities from the total assets, and write the difference on the correct line.

✔ Math Check

Add the total liabilities and the net worth together. That amount should equal the total assets. If not, go back and check your calculations.

5. File Form 1 behind the Forms tab in your file folder, or save your document as TMB_NETW on the Data CD.

Notice how Tyra's assets are greater than her liabilities. It's important for the assets amount to be higher, ideally more than double. Otherwise, Tyra would owe more money than she has.

CHECKPOINT

What is Tyra's most valuable asset? What is her greatest liability?

Planning Tyra's Budget

Next, Tyra and Celina planned a budget based on Tyra's income, the money she earns from her job. They started by using a recent **paycheck stub** (Illustration 1) to see how much money she takes home each month. Follow along by removing Form 2 from page 53 in the *Forms and Documents* section, or by accessing BUDGET on your Data CD. Be sure to put Tyra's name in the heading.

Monthly Income

1. Transfer the amount of monthly Gross Pay shown on the paycheck stub to the line marked *Gross Pay* in the upper section of the budget worksheet. **Gross pay** is the total earned before taxes and other deductions have been subtracted.
2. Add the amounts for taxes and deductions shown on the paycheck stub, and record the total on the line marked *Taxes/ Deductions.*
3. Deduct the amount for Taxes/Deductions from the amount for Gross Pay, and record the final amount on the line marked *Net Pay*. **Net pay** is the amount of money you take home after taxes and other deductions have been removed.

✔ Math Check

The amount of Net Pay plus all taxes and deductions should equal Gross Pay.

Illustration 1: Tyra's Paycheck Stub for August

Water Point Grille — **Earnings Statement**

5101 Lakeland Blvd.
Maplewood, OH 44921

Check Issued: 9/1/--
Pay Period: 8/1/-- to 8/31/--
Tyra M. Burns
4500 Red Maple Lane, Apt. 115
Maplewood, OH 44920
SSN: 333-22-8888

	This Period	Year-to-Date
Gross Pay	$2,700.00	$21,600.00
Deductions		
Federal Income Tax	296.25	2,370.00
Social Security Tax	167.40	1,339.20
State Income Tax	75.00	600.00
City Income Tax	70.20	561.60
Medicare Tax	39.15	313.20
Health Insurance	135.00	1,080.00
Net Pay	$1,917.00	$15,336.00

Now that Tyra knows she has $1,917.00 to work with each month, she can start planning how to spend and save it.

CHECKPOINT

How do you calculate net pay?

Monthly Expenses

Celina explained to Tyra that she should fill out the expense categories in the lower portion of the worksheet using real information taken from old receipts and bills. Tyra pointed out that some expenses change each month. Celina told Tyra that she should **average** her expenses for the categories that vary.

To find the average of a category, Tyra adds up all the amounts in the category. Then she divides the total by the number of amounts she added. The result is a "typical" amount for that category. For example, Tyra's phone bill varies each month, depending on how many long-distance calls she makes. To find the average amount she spends per month for phone service, she could add up all her monthly phone bills for last year (12 months). Then divide the total by 12 months.

Tyra also pointed out that some expenses are required, like rent, while others are her choice, like eating out. For expenses that are her choice, Celina advised her to record an amount she would like to spend for each category, being as realistic as possible. If her planned spending turns out to be more than her income, she will have to go back and adjust her budget by reducing the amounts she can spend in these categories.

FYI *In addition to old bills and receipts, you can use your checkbook register to locate information about your spending.*

Continue using Form 2 to follow along as Tyra fills out her budget worksheet. Here's how Tyra figured out each category:

1. **Savings/Debt Payoff.** Since this is the category that Tyra wanted to change the most, she put down $150.00 as her goal. Enter $150.00 for Savings Accounts under *Savings/Debt Payoff.*
2. **Home.** Tyra knows she spends $450.00 a month on rent. Her average gas and electric bill is $45.00, and her average phone bill is $40.00. Enter these amounts on the correct lines under *Home*. Since Tyra does not spend money on the other categories shown on the form, you can enter a zero or leave those lines blank.
3. **Food/Sundries.** Tyra estimates she spends an average of $50.00 a week, or a total of $200.00 per month, on food and sundries. **Sundries** are small personal items, such as toothpaste and shampoo, or small items for your home, such as light bulbs and paper towels. She decided to divide up this total into these categories: $130.00 for food, $45.00 for personal items, and $25.00 for home care items. Enter these amounts on the correct lines.
4. **Personal.** Tyra decided to set aside $150.00 for clothing and shoes, $75.00 for salon services such as haircuts and manicures. She sets aside $40.00 for dry cleaning and using the coin-operated laundry machines. Enter these amounts on the correct lines.
5. **Transportation.** Tyra gives her parents $200.00 a month to pay off her car. Her car insurance is $120.00 a month, and she thinks she spends about $100.00 on gasoline and oil. Tyra isn't sure how much she should set aside for maintenance. She doesn't have to make repairs very often, but Celina pointed out that when tune-ups and new tires come along, they're expensive. Tyra decided to set aside a sizable amount of $50.00 monthly so that she would be prepared for big car maintenance expenses. She also decided to set aside $7.00 per month to save up for once-a-year license and registration fees. Enter these amounts on the correct lines.
6. **Entertainment.** Celina explained that this category includes such expenses as eating out, movie tickets, dates, and sporting events. Tyra decided to set aside $100.00 for restaurant

meals and $40.00 for events, but nothing for travel expenses. Enter these amounts on the appropriate lines.

7. **Miscellaneous.** At first Tyra did not think she needed any money here, but Celina pointed out how many greeting cards and gifts she buys each year. Tyra decided to set aside $25.00 for gifts, and then added another $15.00 for hobbies. Tyra also remembered that her bank charges a $10.00 fee each month for her checking account. Enter these amounts on the correct lines.
8. **Health Care.** Tyra is very fortunate to have health insurance that helps her pay her medical costs, which could become very expensive if she should get sick or need an operation. Her employer pays part of the insurance **premium**, the regular payment required for an insurance policy. The rest of the premium is deducted from Tyra's paycheck. Tyra's health insurance plan is called a **health maintenance organization (HMO)**. Under this plan, the insurance company pays for most of her medical expenses. When she needs to go to the doctor, she pays only a small fee, called a **copayment**, of $25.00. Her copayment for prescription medicine is $10.00. In her budget, Tyra decided to set aside $15.00 for each of these two categories in case she needs medical care sometime. Enter these figures on the correct lines.

✔ Math Check

After filling out her expenses, Tyra totaled the amounts in each category and in each column, finally arriving at a grand total for all categories. She found she was planning to spend $1,847.00 each month. Total Tyra's expenses for yourself to see if the answers on your form match hers.

9. According to Tyra's paycheck stub, she brings home $1,917.00, or $70.00 more than her planned spending. She can choose to spend or save this money. Since saving is important to Tyra, she decided to increase her savings goal from $150.00 to $220.00. Enter this change on the budget worksheet and adjust your totals. Now her total planned spending and saving should equal her monthly net pay of $1,917.00.
10. File Tyra's final budget worksheet behind the *Forms* tab in your file folder, or save your document as TMB_BUDG.

Now Tyra has a plan for spending and saving. Let's go through one month of her financial activities to see how well she stays within this budget.

CHECKPOINT

What adjustment did Tyra make to her budget when she realized that the total of what she was planning to save and spend in a month was less than her monthly income?

Recording Tyra's Transactions

Celina explained that the key to keeping track of money is to record every transaction in one master record. A **transaction** is any event that involves money coming in or going out. To see how this works, you are going to record all of Tyra's transactions for October in a *Financial Record Book* or in a similar computer file. This ongoing activity will show you exactly how much money she has on any given day, and it will also help you see if Tyra stays within her budget.

Look at the *Financial Record Book*, or open the file called FINREC on your Data CD. Read the headings across the top. For every transaction, record the date and a brief description of the transaction. Use a pencil if you are not working with a computer file. Record all deposits in the *Deposit* column, but record payments under the proper budget categories. For example, if Tyra buys some new clothes, record the cost of the clothes under the *Personal* category.

The last step in recording each transaction is to add the deposit or subtract the payment from the amount in the *Balance* column. The result

Illustration 2: A Filled-Out Financial Record

	Date	Description	Deposit	Savings/Debt Payoff	Home	Food/Sundries	Personal	Transportation	Entertainment	Miscellaneous	Health Care	Balance
1	10/1	Opening Balance										830 12
2	10/2	Wages	1,917 00									2,747 12
3	10/3	Rent (Valley Apartments)			450 00							2,297 12
4												

is the current balance—the total amount in the account after the transaction. Record the current balance in the *Balance* column on the same line as the transaction. Illustration 2 shows how parts of Tyra's filled-out financial record should look.

As you work through each day in Tyra's month, you will work with receipts and other papers. After each work session of recording transactions, file the receipts and papers behind the proper tabs in your file folder. If you are using the Data CD, save this file as TMB_FINR. Then, check off the box next to each day you've completed so you will know which transactions you've recorded.

CHECKPOINT

What is a transaction?

October Transactions

☐ Activities for October 1

1. Open the first page of the *Financial Record Book* or the TMB_FINR file. In the *Balance* column of the first line, enter Tyra's total amount of "spendable money." It is $830.12 ($740.12 in checking + $90.00 in cash). Record the date as 10/1 and the description as Opening Balance. Because this amount is not a deposit, but merely the starting point of Tyra's new system, record the amount only in the *Balance* column. Your form should look like Illustration 2, line 1.

   The amount of money Tyra has in her checking account should also be recorded in her checkbook register. Find the checkbook included in this simulation package. On the first page of the checkbook register, enter $740.12 in the upper-right corner labeled *Balance Fwd* to indicate that this amount is Tyra's current balance, or total amount in the account at this time. Your checkbook register should show the $740.12 recorded as in Illustration 3 below.

Illustration 3:
A Filled-Out Checkbook Register

	CHECK NUMBER	DATE	DESCRIPTION OF TRANSACTION	PAYMENT/ DEBIT (–)	FEE (–)	✓	DEPOSIT/ CREDIT (+)	BALANCE FWD $ 740 12
1	DEP	10/2	Wages	$			$1,917 00	1,917 00
2								2,657 12
3	101	10/3	Valley Apartments	450 00				450 00
4								2,207 12

FINANCIAL RECORD CATEGORIES

Savings/Debt Payoff
Savings Accounts
Investments
Loan Payments

Home
Rent/Mortgage Payment
Property Taxes
Utilities (gas, electric, water, etc)
Phone/Pager Services
Cable/Satellite TV Service
Internet Service
Home Maintenance
Home/Renter's Insurance
Home Furnishings (furniture, appliances, dishes, towels, etc.)
Home Electronics (TV, computer, game system, etc.)

Food/Sundries
Food (prepared and eaten at home)
Personal Care Items (shampoo, soap, toothpaste, etc.)
Small Home Care Items (light bulbs, dishwashing liquid, etc.)

Personal
Clothes & Shoes
Haircuts/Salon Services
Dry Cleaning/Laundry
Gym Membership
Life Insurance

Transportation
Car Loan Payment
Car Insurance
Gasoline/Oil
Car Maintenance (oil change, tires, car washes, etc.)
License/Registration Fees
Bus/Subway Fares

Entertainment
Restaurant Meals (meals, snacks, and beverages; sit-down, take-out, drive-thru, etc.)
Event Fees/Tickets (movies, sporting events, etc.)
Travel Expenses (campgrounds, motels, hotels, airline tickets, rental cars, etc.)

Miscellaneous
Child Care Expenses
Gifts
Donations/Charities
Pet/Hobby Expenses
Education Fees
Bank Service Charges

Health Care
Doctor & Dental Fees
Prescription Medicines
Glasses/Contact Lenses

☐ Activities for October 2

2. Tyra's monthly paycheck is Form 3, pages 55–56 in the *Forms and Documents* section of this instruction book. Deposit this paycheck into her checking account.
   a. Detach the paycheck from the earnings statement (paycheck stub) by cutting or neatly tearing along the dotted lines. Pretend to be Tyra and endorse the paycheck by using a pen to sign it with Tyra's signature, as shown in Illustration 4.
   b. Remove a deposit ticket from the back of the checkbook.
   c. Fill out the deposit ticket by entering the date, bank number from the paycheck, amount, and total, as shown in Illustration 5. (Write the last two numbers of the current year instead of the dashes shown in the illustration.)

Illustration 4:
A Paycheck Endorsed for Deposit Only

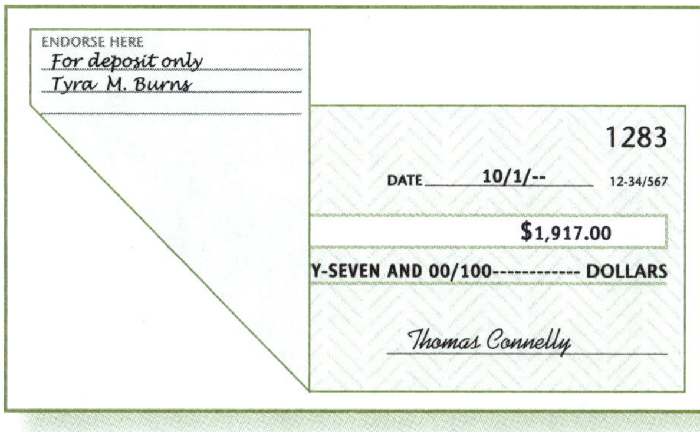
ENDORSE HERE
For deposit only
Tyra M. Burns

1283
DATE 10/1/-- 12-34/567
$1,917.00
Y-SEVEN AND 00/100----------- DOLLARS
Thomas Connelly

Illustration 5:
A Filled-Out Deposit Ticket for a Check Deposit

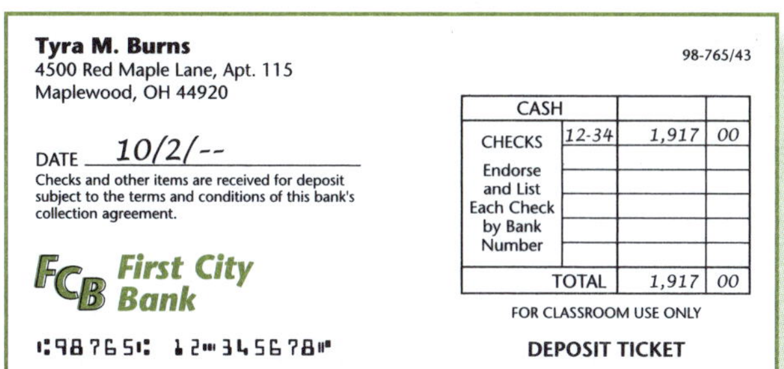
Tyra M. Burns
4500 Red Maple Lane, Apt. 115
Maplewood, OH 44920

98-765/43

DATE 10/2/--
Checks and other items are received for deposit subject to the terms and conditions of this bank's collection agreement.

First City Bank

CASH			
CHECKS	12-34	1,917	00
Endorse and List Each Check by Bank Number			
TOTAL		1,917	00

FOR CLASSROOM USE ONLY
DEPOSIT TICKET

⑆98765⑆ 12⑈345678⑈

The bank number is the hyphenated number in the upper-right corner of the check. Tyra's checking account number is already on the deposit ticket.

d. File the paycheck stub behind the *Receipts* tab in the file folder. File the endorsed paycheck and deposit ticket behind the *Deposits* tab.

Record Tyra's paycheck deposit in the checkbook register. Write the letters "DEP" under *Check Number* to indicate that this is a deposit, not a written check. Enter the date as 10/2 and the description as Wages. Write the amount, $1,917.00, in the *Deposit* column and in the *Balance* column. (It is copied in the *Balance* column to make adding easier.) Add this amount to the previous balance, and record the total as the current balance in the *Balance* column. Your checkbook register should look like Illustration 3, lines 1 and 2.

Record Tyra's paycheck deposit on line 2 in the *Financial Record Book* or the TMB_FINR file. Enter the date as 10/2, the description as Wages, and the deposit amount as $1,917.00. Add this amount to the previous balance, and enter the new total in the *Balance* column. Your form should look like Illustration 2, line 2.

CHECKPOINT

How much money does Tyra have to spend after she deposits her paycheck?

☐ Activities for October 3

3. Tyra's rent is due anytime between the 1st and the 5th of each month. Remove check 101 from the checkbook to pay Tyra's rent. Use a pen when filling out checks.
   a. Fill in the date in the upper-right corner.
   b. Make the check payable to Valley Apartments.
   c. Next to the $ sign, write the amount, $450.00, using numerals. On the *Dollars* line, write the dollar amount in words and the cents as a fraction of a dollar (100 cents). Use the word "and" only to separate the dollars from the cents. For example, $135.26 would be written as one hundred thirty-five and 26/100.
   d. On the line marked *Memo,* write Rent.
   e. Sign the check with Tyra's signature.

Your check should look like Illustration 6. File the filled-out check behind the *Checks Written* tab in the file folder.

Record Tyra's rent payment in the checkbook register. Enter the check number as 101 and the

Illustration 6:
A Filled-Out Check

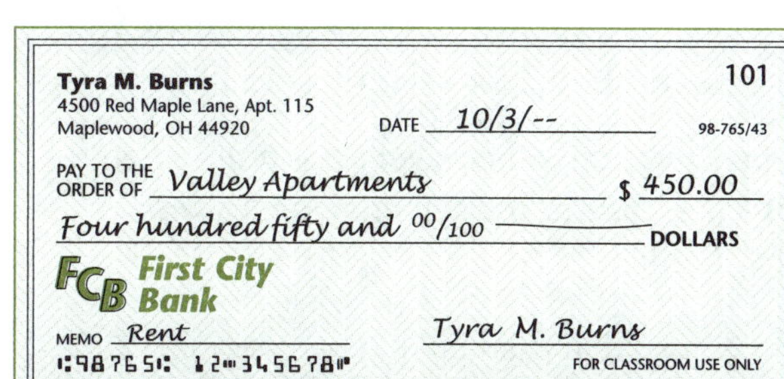
Tyra M. Burns
4500 Red Maple Lane, Apt. 115
Maplewood, OH 44920

101
DATE 10/3/-- 98-765/43

PAY TO THE ORDER OF Valley Apartments $ 450.00
Four hundred fifty and 00/100 DOLLARS

First City Bank

MEMO Rent
Tyra M. Burns
⑆98765⑆ 12⑈345678⑈
FOR CLASSROOM USE ONLY

date as 10/3. In the *Description* section, write the name of the check's payee. The **payee** is the person or business to whom the check is written. For this transaction, the payee is Valley Apartments. Write the amount, $450.00, in the *Payment* column and in the *Balance* column. (Like deposits, payments are also recorded in the *Balance* column of the checkbook register to make subtracting easier.) Subtract this amount from the previous balance, and enter the current balance in the *Balance* column. This transaction in your checkbook register should look like Illustration 3, lines 3 and 4.

Record Tyra's rent payment on line 3 in the *Financial Record Book* or the TMB_FINR file. Enter the date as 10/3 and the description as Rent (Valley Apartments). Record the amount, $450.00, under the *Home* column. Subtract this amount from the previous balance, and enter the difference as the current balance in the *Balance* column. This transaction on your form should look like Illustration 2, line 3.

☐ Activities for October 5

4. When Tyra arrives home from work, she decides to check on the two bills she knows are waiting to be paid. The gas and electric bill (Form 4 on page 55 in the *Forms and Documents* section) for $42.53 is due on 10/10, and the phone bill (Form 5, page 57) for $35.95 is due on 10/12. She decides to pay them now so her payments won't be late.

   Using the same directions as before, write checks 102 and 103 to pay these bills. However, when you write checks to pay bills, always write the account number on the *Memo* line of the check. You can find the account number printed on the bill. This practice will help your money get to the right place. Your checks should look like those in Illustration 7.

FYI ***When you sign a check, your signature should look the same as the signature on file with your bank.***

   Notice that each bill has two sections. Directions on the bill tell you to detach one section and return it with your check. In this simulation, file those sections with the filled-out checks behind the *Checks Written* tab in the file folder. You should keep the other part of each bill as your receipt. File the receipt portion behind the *Receipts* tab in the file folder.

   Following the earlier directions, record these two checks in the checkbook register. Be sure to check your math after subtracting the amounts from the previous balance.

   Finally, following the directions given before, record these two transactions in the *Financial Record Book* or the TMB_FINR file. Refer to the list on page 9 whenever you are unsure about which column to use. You can also find this reference list printed at the front of your *Financial Record Book*. Be sure to check your math when you subtract the amounts from the total.

Illustration 7:
Two Filled-Out Check, Including Billing Account Numbers

Tyra M. Burns
4500 Red Maple Lane, Apt. 115
Maplewood, OH 44920
102
DATE 10/5/--
98-765/43
PAY TO THE ORDER OF Tri-County Gas & Electric $ 42.53
Forty-two and 53/100 DOLLARS
First City Bank
MEMO Acct No. 248-2A
Tyra M. Burns
FOR CLASSROOM USE ONLY

Tyra M. Burns
4500 Red Maple Lane, Apt. 115
Maplewood, OH 44920
103
DATE 10/5/--
98-765/43
PAY TO THE ORDER OF Maplewood Telephone Co. $ 35.95
Thirty-five and 95/100 DOLLARS
First City Bank
MEMO Acct No. 1-419-555-2010
Tyra M. Burns
FOR CLASSROOM USE ONLY

CHECKPOINT

When writing a check what does the term payee mean?

☐ Activities for October 6

5. Tyra stops at the post office to buy stamps. She pays $11.40 in cash. Record the payment in the *Food/Sundries* column in the *Financial Record Book* or the TMB_FINR file. This is a cash transaction; so do not record it in the checkbook register. File the receipt (Form 6, page 57) in the file folder.

☐ Activities for October 8

6. Tyra needs to dress nicely for work, so she goes to the mall to buy a new outfit. She likes the expensive designer clothes, but she remembers her budget and decides to buy some things that are on sale. Her total purchase is $149.46.

   Write check 104 for $149.46 to Park Department Stores. Record the transaction in both the checkbook register and the *Financial Record Book* or the TMB_FINR file. File the receipt (Form 7, page 57) and the check in the correct file folder sections.

7. On her way home, Tyra goes to her favorite small grocery store, Li's Market. Tyra pays $40.80 in cash. Record the transaction in the *Financial Record Book* or the TMB_FINR file, and file the receipt (Form 8 on page 59).

☐ Activities for October 9

8. Tyra wants to get a debit card from her bank. A **debit card** works like a check. She can use it to pay for purchases at many stores. It also enables her to use an **automated teller machine (ATM)** to make deposits to and withdrawals from her checking account without going inside the bank. So Tyra goes to her bank, First City Bank, to fill out the debit card application. Remove Form 9, page 59, and fill out Tyra's application.
   a. Enter Tyra's name, address, phone number, and Social Security number. Refer to page 4.
   b. Complete the form using the following information. Tyra has worked as the restaurant assistant manager at the Water Point Grille for 2 years, 3 months. The phone number for the restaurant is (419) 555-6222. Tyra's checking account number is 12-345678 and her mother's maiden name is Diaz.
   c. Sign Tyra's signature and date the application.

   When Tyra turns in the application, the teller says she should receive the card in about a week. File the application behind the *Forms* tab in the file folder.

FYI ***You can do more than withdraw cash and make deposits at the ATM. You can check your account balances and transfer funds between your accounts. At some ATMs you can buy postage stamps.***

9. While she's at the bank, Tyra asks the teller to withdraw $150 in cash from her checking account. Do not record this transaction in the *Financial Record Book* or the TMB_FINR file because Tyra is neither depositing nor spending any money at this point. But since this does change her checking account balance, record the transaction in the checkbook register as a withdrawal. Write the letters "WD" under *Check Number* to indicate a withdrawal. Record the date and write Withdrawal in the description section. Record $150.00 in the Payment/Debit column and subtract it from the previous balance. File the withdrawal receipt, Form 10 on page 61, behind the *Receipts* tab in the file folder.

   You have completed the first page of the check register. To start a new page, copy the current balance from the bottom of the first page to the *Balance Fwd* column in the upper right corner of the next page.

CHECKPOINT

Why does Tyra need to write the cash withdrawal in her check register but not in the *Financial Record Book* or the TMB_FINR file?

☐ Activities for October 11

10. Tyra and her friends go to a basketball game at the local college. She pays $10.00 in cash for the ticket, but she doesn't get a receipt. Record the transaction in the *Financial Record Book* or the TMB_FINR file, and file the ticket stub (Form 11, page 61) as a receipt in the file folder.

☐ Activities for October 12

11. Tyra goes to her dermatologist for a checkup. Because of her HMO insurance through her job, her copayment is $25.00. Write a check to John Rasgotra, M.D. and record the transaction in both records. File the receipt (Form 12, page 61) and the check in the file folder.

☐ Activities for October 13

12. A few weeks ago, Tyra's friend Lucy asked if Tyra would be willing to sell her old skis. Now that Tyra has thought it over, she's decided to sell the skis because she doesn't go skiing very often and she would rather have the cash. They agree on a price of $85.00.

    Record the $85.00 cash from Lucy as a deposit in the *Financial Record Book* or the TMB_FINR file, because the transaction represents cash coming in. Since she has not yet deposited the money in her checking account, do not record the transaction in the checkbook register.

☐ Activities for October 15

13. It is time for Tyra to send her monthly car payment to her parents. Write a check for $200.00 to Lydia D. Burns. Record the transaction in both record books. File the receipt from Tyra's mother (Form 13, page 63) and the check in the file folder.

☐ Activities for October 17

14. Tyra's debit card (Illustration 8) arrived in today's mail. A letter she received a few days ago assigned her **personal identification number (PIN)**—her "secret code" that allows no one but Tyra to use the card. Her PIN is 0101. She decides to use the card to deposit the $85.00 she received from selling her skis. Pretend you are Tyra making the deposit at the ATM. The machine looks similar to Illustration 9.
    a. Remove a deposit ticket from the back of your checkbook and fill it out as before, except enter $85.00 on the line for cash. Your deposit ticket should look like Illustration 10.
    b. In Illustration 9, locate the slot for inserting your card and imagine that you are inserting it.

Illustration 8:
A Debit Card

Illustration 9:
Parts of an ATM

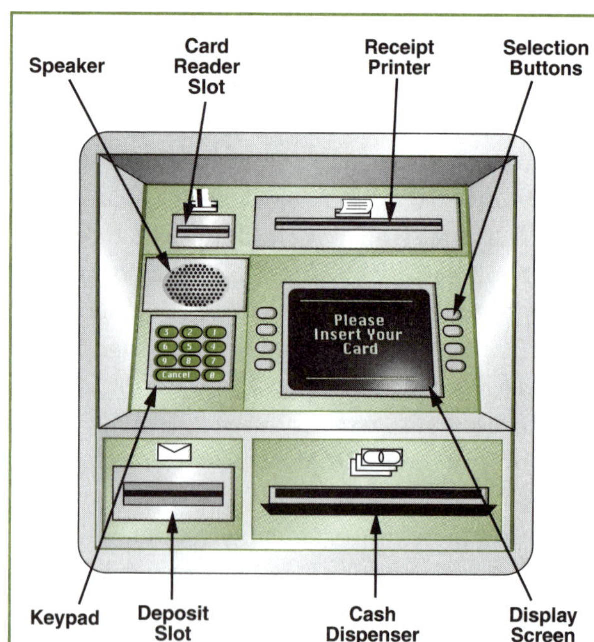

Illustration 10:
A Filled-Out Deposit Ticket for a Cash Deposit

Tyra M. Burns
4500 Red Maple Lane, Apt. 115
Maplewood, OH 44920

98-765/43

DATE 10/17/--

Checks and other items are received for deposit subject to the terms and conditions of this bank's collection agreement.

CASH		85	00
CHECKS			
Endorse and List Each Check by Bank Number			
TOTAL		85	00

FCB First City Bank

FOR CLASSROOM USE ONLY

⑆98765⑆ 12⑈345678⑈

DEPOSIT TICKET

c. When the machine asks for your PIN, key in 0101.
d. When the machine asks what type of transaction you are making, choose Deposit from the menu of choices.
e. When the machine asks what account you are using, choose Checking from the menu of choices.
f. When the machine asks the amount of your transaction, key in 85.00 and press Enter or OK.
g. When the machine asks if you would like a receipt, answer Yes.
h. When the machine is ready to receive the envelope with the deposit inside, a slot will open so you can insert the envelope into the machine. (If you were to actually make this deposit using an ATM, you would seal the money and the deposit ticket in an envelope provided at the machine.)
i. The machine prints out a receipt and returns your card.

FYI *Different machines use different procedures, but the screen messages will always guide you through the correct steps.*

Since you have already recorded this money as a deposit in the *Financial Record Book* or the TMB_FINR file, you will not record it again. However, since it is now in the checking account, and no longer just cash, record the transaction in the checkbook register. In the *Description* column, write ATM Deposit.

Look at the balance shown on the ATM receipt (Form 14, page 63). It does not match the balance in your checkbook register. Why? Tyra gave her parents her car payment two days ago. They probably cashed or deposited the $200.00 check at their bank. Their bank will then return the check to Tyra's bank so that the amount can be subtracted from her account. Tyra's bank has not yet received the check, so the $200.00 still appears in her balance for now. File the ATM receipt behind the *Deposits* tab in the file folder.

One important note: Whether you're making a deposit or withdrawal, some banks will charge you a **service charge**, or fee, for using their ATMs. If the machine warns you that you will be charged a fee for the service, be sure to record that amount as a payment in your checkbook register.

☐ Activities for October 18

15. While driving to a friend's house, Tyra fills her car's gas tank. She pays $34.83 in cash. Record the transaction and file the receipt (Form 15, page 63).

☐ Activities for October 19

16. On her way home from work, Tyra stops at the supermarket for groceries. She uses three coupons (labeled as Form 16 on page 65) for items she was planning to purchase, so her total cost is $53.28. Pretend you are Tyra using the debit card to pay for the groceries.
    a. Slide the card through the machine near the checkout register.
    b. Press the ATM Card button.
    c. Enter the PIN given in Step 14.
    d. When the machine asks "Is 53.28 correct?" press Enter or Yes.

When you make a purchase with a debit card, the amount is immediately withdrawn from your checking account and transferred to the store's account. Record the debit transaction in both the checkbook register and the *Financial Record Book* or the TMB_FINR file. In the checkbook register, write the letters "DBT" under *Check Number* to indicate a debit transaction. Then file the receipt (Form 17, page 65) in the proper place.

CHECKPOINT

What is a PIN and what do the letters "PIN" stand for?

☐ Activities for October 21

17. Tyra takes her car in for an oil change for $33.96. However, she accidentally writes the wrong amount of money on the check. To correct her error, she must **void** the check, which is a special process of destroying the check so that no one can cash it. To void a check, write VOID in large letters across the check. Record the check number and date in your checkbook register and write VOID in the description section. Do not record the amount. Instead, draw lines through the Balance space for the voided check. Then start over with a new check.

    Write check 107 to Zhang's Garage for the incorrect amount of $23.96. Then void the check. Follow Illustration 11. Write a new check (check 108) for the correct amount. Record the transaction, and file both checks and the receipt (Form 18, page 67).

Illustration 11:
A Voided Check

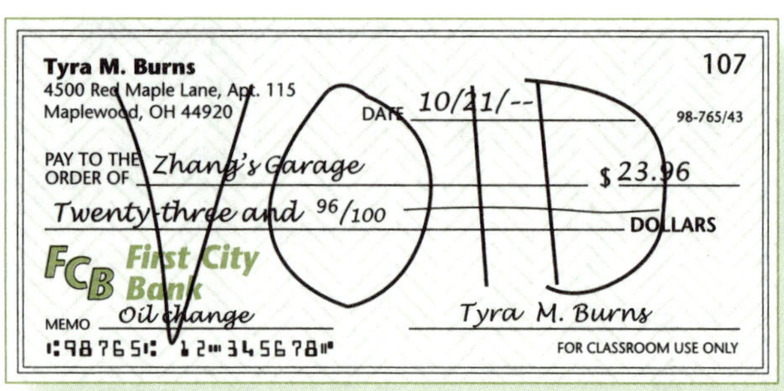

☐ Activities for October 22

18. Tyra's nephew, Will, is turning two next weekend, and she wants to buy him a gift. Before she goes to the store, she checks her budget sheet and sees that her spending limit is $25. At the store, she decides to buy a puzzle, for a total cost plus tax of $19.49. Write a check to Tally Toys, record the transaction, and file the check and receipt (Form 19, page 67).

☐ Activities for October 23

19. A few days ago, Tyra received her car insurance bill (Form 20, page 69), which is due on 10/30. She decides to pay it today. Write a check to Latero Insurance for $120.00. Record the transaction. Then file the receipt and the check with the correct portion of the bill.

☐ Activities for October 25

20. After work Tyra heads to Harper's Salon to get her hair cut and colored. She pays $63.00, plus $10.00 for a tip. Record a cash transaction of $73.00. On the receipt (Form 21, page 69), note the $10.00 tip on the bottom so you won't forget the amount, and file the receipt.

☐ Activities for October 28

21. A few weeks ago, Tyra and her friend Lela decided to go to dinner and to the ballet. When Lela called to reserve the tickets she was told that the tickets would be at the Will Call window. On the way to pick up Lela, Tyra stops at the ATM to get cash for dinner and her ticket. She has about $70.00 in her wallet, but she knows that is not enough, so she withdraws $150.00 from the machine. Record the ATM withdrawal in the checkbook register, and file the ATM receipt (Form 22, page 69) under *Receipts*.

22. Tyra and Lela get separate checks. Tyra's dinner costs $29.36. She gives the server $35.00 and tells him to keep the change, $5.64, for his tip. When they arrive at the Civic Center, Tyra spends $70.00 for her ticket to the ballet and $5.00 for a souvenir program. Record these cash transactions in the *Financial Record Book* only. (You recorded the withdrawal from checking earlier.) Note the tip on the bottom of the restaurant receipt and file all the receipts (Form 23, page 71).

☐ Activities for October 29

23. Tyra reviews her budget and realizes she is within her limits in every category. To transfer her goal amount to her savings account, Tyra writes a check to herself for $220.00. Write the check and record it in the checkbook register. Then use Form 24, page 71, to deposit the money in Tyra's savings account (#12-999999). Illustration 12 shows Tyra's updated savings account balance. Since the amount is no longer "spendable money," record the check as a payment to *Savings* in the *Financial Record Book.* Under *Description,* write Transfer to Savings. File the savings deposit form and check in the file folder.

Now that Tyra has proven to herself that she can live within her budget limits, she wants to make setting aside her savings goal a top priority. In the future, she will transfer money from her checking account to her savings account at the beginning of the month, just after she receives her paycheck.

☐ Activities for October 31

24. Since it is the last day of the month, Tyra decides to **reconcile** her checkbook and **prove cash** in her financial record. To reconcile her checkbook, Tyra will determine if her bank's checking account statement matches her own checkbook register. To prove cash, she will verify that her *Financial Record Book* records are accurate.

    Begin this process by removing Tyra's monthly bank statement for October (Form 25, page 73). Find the checkbook register and all of the written checks, deposit tickets, and ATM statements in the file folder. Assume that all of the checks have been processed through the bank, which means they are **canceled checks**. When you reconcile

Illustration 12: Tyra's Savings Account Statement

FCB First City Bank

TYRA M. BURNS
4500 RED MAPLE LANE, APT. 115
MAPLEWOOD, OH 44920

Statement For: 9/29/-- to 10/29/--
Beginning Balance: $69.65
Ending Balance: $289.65
Account Number: 12-999999

Regular Savings Account

Date	Description	Amount	Balance
10/29	DEPOSIT	$220.00	$289.65

Illustration 13: A Checkbook Register Showing a Confirmed Entry

CHECK NUMBER	DATE	DESCRIPTION OF TRANSACTION	PAYMENT/ DEBIT (–)		FEE (–)	✓	DEPOSIT/ CREDIT (+)		BALANCE FWD	
									$ 740	12
DEP	10/2	Wages	$			✓	$1,917	00	1,917	00
									2,657	12
101	10/3	Valley Apartments	450	00					450	00
									2,207	12

your checking account in real life, some checks will probably be **outstanding**. These are checks that have not finished their route from the payee's bank to yours. As a result, your bank has not yet *paid* the checks and subtracted the amounts from your account. Most bank statements show the dates the bank paid the checks, not the dates they were written.

a. Compare your records of deposits against the bank statement (Form 25). The statement shows a deposit of $1,917.00 on 10/2 and a deposit of $85.00 on 10/17. You should have two deposit tickets matching these amounts. Now find these entries in your checkbook register. Place a checkmark in the checkmark column next to the entries. (See Illustration 13 for an example.)
b. Compare your records of written checks, withdrawals, and debit transactions against the bank statement. The statement shows ten canceled checks, two withdrawals, and one debit transaction. You should have canceled checks and receipts for all of these transactions. (Your receipt for the debit transaction is the receipt from Holland's Groceries.) Check off each entry as you confirm that the amounts in all three places match exactly.
c. Record any service charges or fees shown on the statement in the *Fee* column in the checkbook register. First City Bank deducts a $10.00 service charge each month from Tyra's checking account. Enter that amount in the checkbook register in the *Fee* column and code it "SC" for "service charge." Subtract that amount from the balance. Also record the service charge in the *Financial Record Book* or TMB_FINR file under the Miscellaneous category.
d. Now compare the balance in the checkbook register with the balance on the monthly bank statement. These two amounts should match. If not, go back and check your calculations for each entry in the checkbook register until you find your error.

Return all written checks and other documents to the proper places in the file folder.

25. As you have probably figured out by now, the main difference between the checkbook register and the *Financial Record Book* is that the record book involves cash as well as checks. You can check the accuracy of the balance in the *Financial Record Book* or the TMB_FINR file by comparing it to the sum of cash Tyra has now plus the balance in her checking account. The ending balance in the record book should equal the ending balance in her checking account plus the cash in her wallet.

✔ Math Check

Add Tyra's current cash ($109.97) to her checking account balance ($1,082.45). Does this sum equal the balance in the *Financial Record Book* or TMB_FINR file? If not, go back and check your calculations in the record book to find your error. Keep in mind that the $220.00 deposited into her savings account should not be added back at this stage since it is no longer "spendable" money.

26. As the last step, total each of the payment columns in the *Financial Record Book* or the TMB_FINR file. Write the totals in the boxes at the bottom of each column. Compare these amounts to Tyra's original budget sheet and note that she has stayed within budget in every category.

CHECKPOINT

When do you place a checkmark in the checkbook register next to an entry for a check?

Planning and Money Management

Standard 2: *Develop a plan for spending and saving.*

It is never too early to develop a plan for spending and saving. You can start planning by thinking about where you get money and how you spend it. If you have a job or get an allowance, you should be thinking about your relationship with money.

Even if you don't have regular income from an allowance or a job, you can think about the money you receive as gifts, cash you get from family members, and money you earn doing chores or occasional work such as mowing lawns and babysitting.

Activities

1. Explain how Tyra's experience might help you begin to develop a plan for spending and saving.
2. Ask a family member to explain the benefits of developing a plan for spending and saving. Ask if they have any tips they can share. Use a bulleted list to summarize your conversation.

Special Topics

Locate the following Special Topic readings on the Data CD. Read the article and answer the Think It Through questions that appear at the end of the article.

- Special Topic 4: How a Budget Puts You in Control
- Special Topic 5: Where Does All the Money Go?
- Special Topic 6: Saving for Something Special

Part 3 Raising a Family

Performance Outcomes

In this part of the simulation, you will learn to:

1. Prepare a statement of net worth and a budget for a single working parent.
2. Understand the difference between good debt and bad debt.
3. Pay bills and make purchases online.
4. Use a credit card properly.
5. Figure federal income taxes for a single working parent.
6. Apply for a car loan.
7. Use the Internet to research a major purchase.
8. Adjust a budget to allow for a major purchase.
9. Use an interest-bearing checking account.
10. Continue developing solid financial management skills, such as record keeping and decision making.

MEET ADAM G. WARNER

© Fotosearch, Comstock

Adam G. Warner is 30 years old. He has a full-time job, and he is raising his three-year-old son, Carson, by himself.

About eight years ago, Adam earned a bachelor's degree in sociology. In his first few working years, he held several different jobs. But five years ago Adam began working for a small company called Cabot Services, a property management company. Cabot has grown rapidly since then, so Adam's job duties as human resource manager have grown, too. Although his job can be stressful, Adam enjoys contributing to the careers and lives of other Cabot employees. Adam earns an annual salary of $60,000, and is paid semi-monthly (twice a month). His Social Security number is 111-55-9999.

At home, Adam and Carson live in a two-bedroom townhouse at 4412 Lincoln Avenue in Hopewell, Ohio 45313. Their phone number is (937) 555-2262. Adam pays $900.00 a month in rent, which includes water and trash collection. He pays for gas and electricity, telephone, and cable Internet and TV services separately. One of Adam's biggest expenses is child care for his son, but he knows that providing a safe place for Carson is worth every penny. Adam and Carson are fairly comfortable, but Adam knows he's going to have to buy a new car soon. He has some money saved, but not enough to pay for a car. He will have to take out a car loan to pay for the difference between the price of a car and the amount of savings he puts toward the purchase. The car he drives now is paid for, so adding a monthly car payment to his expenses will have a major impact on his budget.

CHECKPOINT

How are Adam and Carson Warner related to each other?

Figuring Out Adam's Net Worth

Do you recall filling out Tyra's net worth worksheet in Part 2? Now you can do the same for Adam. Remove Form 26 from page 75 of the *Forms and Documents* section of this instruction book, or call up the NETWORTH_3 file on your data CD.

You may need to refer to the directions on page 3 in Part 2. Use the information shown below to complete Adam's net worth form. Be sure to check your calculations. Then file Form 26 behind the *Forms* tab of the file folder, or save your document as AGW_NETW.

CHECKPOINT

What is the basic calculation for figuring out net worth?

Assets

- $639.27 in an interest-bearing checking account.
- $5,520.81 in a money market savings account.
- $21,148.37 in a 401(k) retirement savings account.
- $1,800.00 cash value of a life insurance policy.
- Current value of his car, $1,700.00.
- Value of his personal items, $4,300.00.
- $180.00 in cash.

Liabilities

- March rent, $900.00.
- Hopewell Energy bill, $105.10.
- PBC Telephone Company bill, $34.31.
- Express Cable Service bill (TV & Internet), $136.95.
- S&T Insurance Company bill (auto, renter's, life), $73.00.

Writing Out Adam's Budget

Adam has been using a budget worksheet to manage his money since he graduated from high school, and he updates it whenever his financial situation changes. Think about how you filled out Tyra's budget worksheet in Part 2. Now fill out Adam's worksheet. Remove Form 27 from page 75 of the *Forms and Documents* section of this instruction book, or open BUDGET on the data CD. Use the budget information on page 21 to complete Adam's current budget.

✔ Math Check

Add up Adam's monthly expenses. Now, look at Illustration 14 on page 23. This is Adam's paycheck receipt (stub). Because Adam receives two paychecks a month (one on the 1st and one on the 15th), his monthly net pay is double what is shown on this paycheck receipt. Does Adam's monthly net pay cover his monthly expenses?

File Adam's budget worksheet behind the *Forms* tab, or save your document as AGW_BUDG.

You will now work through a month's worth of financial transactions for Adam. Check the boxes next to the dates as you complete each day's activities.

CHECKPOINT

Which single item accounts for Adam's largest monthly expense?

ADAM'S BUDGET INFORMATION

Monthly Income (rounded)
Gross Pay, $5,000.00
Taxes/Deductions, $1,525.00
Net Pay, $3,475.00

Savings/Debt Payoff
Savings, $150.00

Home
Rent, $900.00
Utilities, $105.00
Phone Service, $35.00
Cable TV Service, $90.00
Cable Internet Service, $50.00
Renter's Insurance, $16.00

Food/Sundries
Food, $300.00
Personal Care Items, $60.00
Home Care Items, $40.00

Personal
Clothes and Shoes, $400.00
Haircuts, etc., $40.00
Dry Cleaning, Laundry, $30.00
Life Insurance Premium, $12.00

Transportation
Car Insurance Premium, $45.00
Gasoline, $150.00
Maintenance, $85.00
License/Registration, $7.00

Entertainment
Restaurant Meals, $150.00
Event Fees/Tickets, $60.00

Miscellaneous
Child Care, $620.00
Gifts, $75.00
Bank Service Charges, $10.00

Health Care
Doctor and Dental Fees, $25.00
Prescription Medicines, $20.00

March Transactions

☐ Activities for March 1

1. On the first page of the *Financial Record Book* for Part 3, enter Adam's total amount of spendable money ($639.27 in his checking account + $180.00 in cash). Enter the date as 3/1, record the description as Opening balance, and enter the amount in the *Balance* column. Or call up the FINREC document on your data CD, record the

opening balance, and save the document as AGW_FINR.

Start a new page in the checkbook register and enter Adam's balance of $639.27. Refer to Illustration 3 on page 8 in this instruction book to see an example of how a balance is entered in the top right corner of the page.

☐ Activities for March 2

2. Adam arranged with his employer to have his semimonthly paychecks deposited automatically into his checking account. This form of payment is called **direct deposit**. On paydays, Adam receives a receipt for the direct deposit instead of a paycheck. The receipt provides the same information as a paycheck stub. Remove the receipt for Adam's March 1 paycheck (Form 28, page 77), and check that all the information is correct.
   a. Check his name, address, and Social Security number against the information given on page 18 in this instruction book.

Illustration 14: Adam's Paycheck Receipt

Cabot Services, Inc.

8820 Main Street
Hopewell, OH 45311
(937) 555-3777

Adam G. Warner
4412 Lincoln Ave
Hopewell, OH 45313
SSN: 111-55-9999

Direct Deposit Paycheck Receipt
(This is not a check.)

Date Issued: 3/1/--

Amount Deposited: $1,737.51

Pay	This Period	YTD
Gross Pay	$2,500.00	$10,000.00
Net Pay	$1,737.51	$ 6,950.04

Deductions	This Period	YTD
401(k)	$150.00	$600.00
Federal Tax	$231.21	$924.84
State Tax	$ 79.98	$319.92
Soc. Sec.	$155.00	$620.00
Medicare	$ 36.25	$145.00
PPO Health Plan	$110.05	$440.20

Deposited to:

Hopewell Community Bank
Checking account #: 21-436587

b. Adam has chosen to have a portion of each paycheck deposited into a 401(k) account. A **401(k) account** is a special account workers can use to save money, mainly for retirement. You don't have to pay income tax right away on money deposited in a 401(k) account. Your contributions are not taxable until you withdraw the funds, usually at retirement. In most cases, if you withdraw money from your 401(k) account before you reach retirement age, you will have to pay a large financial penalty.

   Adam has chosen to contribute 6% of his salary to a 401(k) account. Check to make sure that this deduction is correct. Assume the other tax deductions are correct.

c. Check that his bank information is correctly stated as Hopewell Community Bank, checking account #21-436587.

FYI *The letters* YTD *on Adam's paycheck receipt stand for* year-to-date. *There is year-to-date information for his pay and for his deductions.*

Record the direct deposit in the *Financial Record Book* or AGW_FINR file and in the checkbook register. File the paycheck receipt behind the *Receipts* tab in the file folder.

CHECKPOINT

Explain the relationship between gross and net pay. Which one is always a smaller amount?

☐ Activities for March 3

3. On his lunch hour, Adam stops to have the oil in his car changed at Easy-Fix Car Care. As the technicians are working on the car, they discover it needs a new air filter and that oil is leaking from somewhere in the car. Adam feels frustrated because nearly everything about his formerly reliable car is now in need of repair. He thanks the technicians for noticing the problem and pays for the service with check 672 for $54.78.

   In this part and in Part 4, you will no longer write checks or deposit tickets. However, you will still need to record the checks and deposits in the checkbook register and in the *Financial Record Book* or AGW_FINR file as directed. Record this transaction in both places. File the receipt (Form 29, page 77) behind the *Receipts* tab in the file folder.

4. Adam's rent isn't due until the 10th day of the month, but he likes to pay early to make sure he doesn't forget and get charged a late fee. Record check 673 for $900.00 to Lakeview Properties (the company that owns his townhouse) in the *Financial Record Book* or AGW_FINR file and in the checkbook register.

☐ Activities for March 4

5. Adam's bills for his gas and electric, telephone, and cable Internet and TV services are all due within the next week. (See Forms 30-32, pages 79-81 of this instruction book.) Two months ago, Adam registered at his bank's Web site so that he could pay these bills online. At the site, he followed the step-by-step instructions to enter the personal and checking account information required to set up the online account. He chose a user ID and PIN (personal identification number) that would identify him as the account holder. He wrote down the ID and PIN and put them in a safe place.

   Then, following instructions at the site, he entered account numbers and addresses for each bill he wanted to pay online. He had to go through this set-up process only once. Now, each month, he can just select the payee (company) and enter the amount of the bill. The bank will deduct that amount from his checking account and pay the bill.

   To pay these bills today, Adam goes to his bank's Internet home page. He follows the same steps to pay each bill, starting with the gas and electric bill. Pretend you are Adam paying bills online. You would use your computer keyboard and mouse to complete these transactions:

a. At the home page, click the link for Online Banking. (Each bank's web site looks different, but the links will be clearly marked and easy to follow.)
b. In the log-in box that appears, enter Adam's user ID: AGW4658 and PIN: 80523, and click Log In. A closed-lock symbol at the bottom of the computer screen tells you that you have entered a secure Web page.
c. Now that Adam has accessed his account, he can view his account balance, review transactions, order checks, or complete other transactions. Today, he wants to pay bills. Click the Make Payments link.
d. Illustration 15 shows the bill payment Web page for Adam's account. Click the down-arrow next to Payee. You will see the list of payees Adam has set up.
e. Click Hopewell Energy, Inc. to select this payee.
f. Enter the payment amount: $105.10.
g. Click OK to transmit the information.
h. The next Web page asks you to review the information you just entered to make sure it is correct. Check to see that you have scheduled the correct payment of $105.10 to Hopewell Energy, Inc.
i. Click Pay to complete the transaction.
j. Repeat the process to pay the phone and cable companies. Be sure to check the payment amounts each time before completing the transaction.
k. When finished, click the Log Out button to end your online session.

Illustration 15: Adam's Online Bill-Payment Page

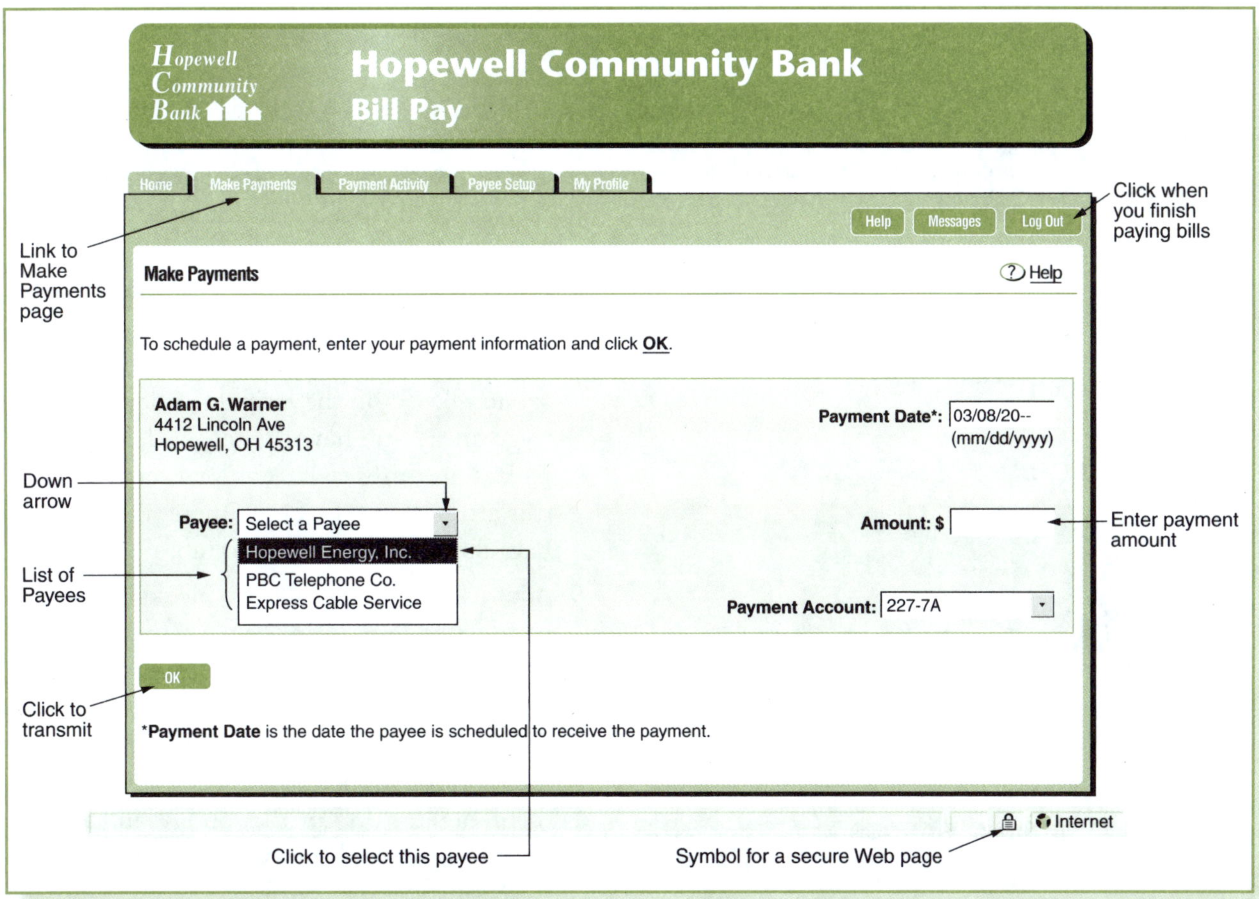

Because all three of these payments are made with money from Adam's checking account, record all three transactions in the *Financial Record Book* or AGW_FINR file and in the checkbook register. In the Check Number column of the checkbook register, write the code ON to indicate a payment made online. In the Description section of the checkbook register and record book, write the name of the payee, just as you would record a check. On each bill, write the date and the amount of the payment and make a note that it was paid online. File the paid bills behind the *Receipts* tab of the file folder.

☐ Activities for March 6

6. Adam has one all-purpose credit card (Illustration 16). To keep his credit card debt under control, he uses the card only for online purchases and for gasoline. He chose a WorldCard because it does not impose a **finance charge** if he pays off the balance in full each month.

   On the way home from work, Adam stops at GasCo to fill his car's gas tank. He uses his credit card to pay $35.24 for the gas. He always saves his receipts so that he can check them against the credit card bill at the end of the month. Record the transaction in the *Financial Record Book* or AGW_FINR file, and file the receipt (Form 33, page 81). Because this is a credit purchase, Adam will not record the transaction in his checkbook register until he pays the credit card bill later by check.

Illustration 16:
Adam's Credit Card

FYI

Having only one credit card helps you control spending. With multiple cards, it is easy to spend more than you can afford.

7. After picking up Carson from the daycare center, Adam stops at the Hilltop Grocery Store. His purchases total $79.33. He uses his debit card to pay for the groceries. Debit card transactions are not credit. The payment amount will be immediately deducted from Adam's checking account. Record the transaction in the *Financial Record Book* or AGW_FINR file and in the checkbook register. File the receipt (Form 34, page 83) in the file folder.

CHECKPOINT

Identify the payee and amounts paid for each of the bills Adam paid online.

☐ Activities for March 8

8. On this Saturday morning, Adam takes his car to his mechanic, Jason Dobbs at Jason's Garage, to check the oil leak. Before leaving the garage, he wisely asks for an **estimate**. This is a written document showing how much a repair or other service is likely to cost. The customer can then decide, before work begins, whether or not to go ahead with the service. Based on the estimate, Adam decides to go ahead and have the car fixed. Mr. Dobbs promises to have the car ready by late this afternoon. File the estimate (Form 35, page 83) behind the *Receipts* tab.
9. Adam and Carson walk two blocks to the park. After an hour in the park, they walk home and eat lunch. While Carson takes a nap, Adam fills out his income tax forms to figure out how much tax he owes the government on the money he earned last year. Tax forms are due on April 15, and Adam doesn't want to wait until the last minute to fill out the forms. Remove Form 36 (pages 85–86)

and follow along as Adam completes this form. Refer to Illustration 17 for information provided by his employer on the W-2 form and by his bank on the 1099-INT form, as needed. Also, refer to the tax tables shown in Illustration 18, on page 28 when directed.

a. Fill out Adam's name, address, and Social Security number from the W-2 form in Illustration 17.

b. In the Filing status section, you must check the one box that best describes Adam's status. Adam is single, but he also

Illustration 17: Adam's W-2 Form and 1099 Form from Last Year

a Employee's social security number 111-55-9999	OMB No. 1545-0008	
b Employer identification number (EIN) 99-0000099	1 Wages, tips, other compensation $54,050.00	2 Federal income tax withheld $5,139.60
c Employer's name, address, and ZIP code Chabot Services, Inc. 8820 Main St Hopemwell, OH 45311	3 Social security wages $57,500.00	4 Social security tax withheld $3,564.96
	5 Medicare wages and tips $57,500.00	6 Medicare tax withheld $833.76
	7 Social security tips	8 Allocated tips
d Control number	9 Advance EIC payment	10 Dependent care benefits
e Employeeís first name and initial / Last name / Suff. Adam G. Warner 4412 Lincoln Ave Hopewell, OH 45313	11 Nonqualified plans	12a See instructions for box 12 Code E $3,450.00
	13 Statutory employee ☐ Retirement plan ☒ Third-party sick pay ☐	12b Code
	14 Other	12c Code
f Employeeís address and ZIP code		12d Code

15 State	Employerís state ID number	16 State wages, tips, etc.	17 State income tax	18 Local wages, tips, etc.	19 Local income tax	20 Locality name
OH	23-5555	$54,050	$1,900.56	$54,050		Hopewell

Form **W-2** Wage and Tax Statement **20__** Department of the TreasuryóInternal Revenue Service

Hopewell Community Bank

Form 1099–INT
Statement of Interest Earned

For: Adam G. Warner, 4412 Lincoln Ave, Hopewell, OH 45313
Social Security Number 111-55-9999

Account Number	Account Type	Interest Earned
21–436587	Interest-bearing checking	$47.20
21–909090	Money Market savings	$123.61

provides a home for a dependent child. A **dependent** is a person who relies on someone else for financial support. Because Tory supports a child, he qualifies as the "head of household." Check box 4.

c. The next section helps you figure out the number of exemptions Adam qualifies for. **Exemptions** reduce the amount of income that will be taxed. So, the more exemptions you are allowed to take, the lower your tax. On line 6a, check the first box for Yourself and write 1 in the box in the right margin. Under 6c, list Carson Warner, Social Security number 634-56-3616, and son. Then check the box to indicate that Carson qualifies for the child tax credit. Write 1 in the second box in the right column because Carson is also an exemption for Adam. On line 6d, write the total number of exemptions, 2, in the right-hand box.

d. In Illustration 17, locate box 1 on the W-2 form. Write this wage amount on line 7 of the tax form.

e. Line 8 refers to the amount of interest that Adam's bank accounts earned last year. Add the two amounts shown on Form 1099 in Illustration 17, and write the figure, $170.81, on line 8a.

f. Lines 8b through 14b don't apply to Adam. Add lines 7 and 8a together and write the amount on line 15.

g. Lines 16 through 19 also do not apply to Adam. Write zero on line 20. Follow the instructions for line 21. Then transfer the number from line 21 ($54,220.81) to line 22 on the top of page 2.

h. Skip lines 23a and 23b because they don't apply to Adam. Read the directions for line 24. Adam is not itemizing his deductions; he will use the standard deduction. Look at Adam's filing status on line 4. Because he qualifies as head of household, his standard deduction is $7,850.00. Write this amount on line 24.

i. Follow the directions on lines 25, 26, and 27, and enter your answers.

j. The answer on line 27 ($39,570.81) is Adam's **taxable income**, the amount of income on which he must pay a tax.

k. To find out how much tax Adam owes, look at Illustration 18. In the left column, locate the range in which Adam's taxable income falls. It is $39,550 to $39,600.

Illustration 18:
Income Tax Tables from the Income Tax Directions Booklet

If line 43 (taxable income) is		And you are—			
At least	But less than	Single	Married filing jointly *	Married filing sepa-rately	Head of a house-hold
		Your tax is—			
38,000					
38,000	**38,050**	5,930	4,921	5,930	5,144
38,050	**38,100**	5,943	4,929	5,943	5,151
38,100	**38,150**	5,955	4,936	5,955	5,159
38,150	**38,200**	5,968	4,944	5,968	5,166
38,200	**38,250**	5,980	4,951	5,980	5,174
38,250	**38,300**	5,993	4,959	5,993	5,181
38,300	**38,350**	6,005	4,966	6,005	5,189
38,350	**38,400**	6,018	4,974	6,018	5,196
38,400	**38,450**	6,030	4,981	6,030	5,204
38,450	**38,500**	6,043	4,989	6,043	5,211
38,500	**38,550**	6,055	4,996	6,055	5,219
38,550	**38,600**	6,068	5,004	6,068	5,226
38,600	**38,650**	6,080	5,011	6,080	5,234
38,650	**38,700**	6,093	5,019	6,093	5,241
38,700	**38,750**	6,105	5,026	6,105	5,249
38,750	**38,800**	6,118	5,034	6,118	5,256
38,800	**38,850**	6,130	5,041	6,130	5,264
38,850	**38,900**	6,143	5,049	6,143	5,271
38,900	**38,950**	6,155	5,056	6,155	5,279
38,950	**39,000**	6,168	5,064	6,168	5,286
39,000					
39,000	**39,050**	6,180	5,071	6,180	5,294
39,050	**39,100**	6,193	5,079	6,193	5,301
39,100	**39,150**	6,205	5,086	6,205	5,309
39,150	**39,200**	6,218	5,094	6,218	5,316
39,200	**39,250**	6,230	5,101	6,230	5,324
39,250	**39,300**	6,243	5,109	6,243	5,331
39,300	**39,350**	6,255	5,116	6,255	5,339
39,350	**39,400**	6,268	5,124	6,268	5,346
39,400	**39,450**	6,280	5,131	6,280	5,354
39,450	**39,500**	6,293	5,139	6,293	5,361
39,500	**39,550**	6,305	5,146	6,305	5,369
39,550	**39,600**	6,318	5,154	6,318	5,376
39,600	**39,650**	6,330	5,161	6,330	5,384
39,650	**39,700**	6,343	5,169	6,343	5,391
39,700	**39,750**	6,355	5,176	6,355	5,399
39,750	**39,800**	6,368	5,184	6,368	5,406
39,800	**39,850**	6,380	5,191	6,380	5,414
39,850	**39,900**	6,393	5,199	6,393	5,421
39,900	**39,950**	6,405	5,206	6,405	5,429
39,950	**40,000**	6,418	5,214	6,418	5,436

Then follow that line across to the right-hand column under *Head of a household*. This amount, $5,376.00, is the amount of tax owed on Adam's taxable income. Write this figure on line 28.

l. **Tax credits** are amounts that taxpayers may subtract from the tax they owe. On the next several lines, you will subtract the tax credits for which Adam qualifies. Adam gets a tax credit because he pays for child care for Carson. On a separate form not shown here, Adam has determined that his credit amount is $600.00. Write this amount on line 29.

m. Adam also qualifies for the child tax credit, line 32. On a separate form not shown here, Adam figured this credit to be $1,000. Write this number on line 32. (Lines 30, 31, and 33 do not apply to Adam.)

n. Follow the directions for lines 34, 35, and 37, and enter your answers on those lines. (Line 36 does not apply to Adam.)

o. Now that his credits have been subtracted, line 37 shows the total tax Adam owes for the year. However, his employer has been taking money out, or **withholding** money, from each paycheck all year long. Cabot Services sends this money to the government as payments on Adam's income taxes. Look at Form W-2 in Illustration 17. The total amount that Cabot withheld for federal income taxes is shown in box 2. Enter the amount, $5,139.60, on lines 38 and 42. (Lines 39–41 do not apply to Adam.)

p. Compare the amount Adam has already paid (line 42) to the tax owed (line 37). Notice that he has paid more than he owes. He will get a **refund** from the government. Find the amount of his refund by subtracting line 37 from line 42. Enter the answer on line 43.

q. Adam decides to have the full amount of his refund deposited directly into his checking account. Fill out lines 44a–44d. Adam called his bank to get the routing number for line 44b: 110593822. His checking account number appears on Form 1099 in Illustration 17.

r. Sign Adam's signature and add the date and his occupation at the bottom of the form. Fill in his daytime (work) phone number, which is his employer's number: (937) 555-3777.

Before Adam mails Form 1040A, along with a copy of his W-2 to the Internal Revenue Service, he makes a copy for himself. On another day before April 15, Adam will have to follow a similar procedure for determining his state income taxes.

In real life, this form and the information you will need to fill it out will change yearly. Although the process will be similar each year, you'll need to follow the instruction booklet that comes with your tax form each time you figure your taxes.

FYI

Not everyone gets a tax refund. If the total tax on line 37 is greater than the total payments on line 42, the taxpayer must pay the difference when the tax form is filed on or before April 15.

10. Around 3:00 in the afternoon, Jason Dobbs calls to say the car is ready to be picked up. The total, with tax, comes to $201.40. The actual bill is less than 10% more than the estimate, so it is reasonable. Adam writes a check for the repairs. Record the transaction in the *Financial Record Book* or AGW_FINR file and in the checkbook register. File the receipt (Form 37, page 87) with the estimate under *Receipts*.

    Before he leaves, Adam asks Mr. Dobbs for his opinion about his car. Mr. Dobbs believes the car will need more and more repairs in the near future. He suggests that perhaps it's time to buy a more reliable car, something Adam expected him to say. He already has been thinking about putting money into payments on a new car, rather than continuing to pay for repairs on the old car.

CHECKPOINT

Calculate the difference between the estimate for repairing Adam's car and the actual amount Adam paid. Did Adam pay more or less than the estimate?

☐ Activities for March 10

11. On his lunch hour, Adam goes to the bank. Alice Littlebear, the loan officer at Hopewell Community Bank, gives Adam a car loan application. Remove Form 38 from page 89 and follow along as Adam fills out this application.

    a. Next to Branch, write Sherwood.
    b. Under Purpose, write Car loan.
    c. Under Amount Requested, write $16,000.00, even though Adam probably won't need to borrow that much.
    d. Under Terms Requested, write the time needed to pay off the loan, which in this case is five years (or 60 months).
    e. Under Applicant Information, find Adam's full name, address, phone number, and Social Security number on page 19 in this instruction book. (County is Trent and Length of Residence is 2 years and 6 months.)
    f. Under Birth Date, write August 28, 19--.
    g. Under No. of Dependents, write 1.
    h. For Previous Residence, write N/A for "not applicable" because Adam has lived at his current residence longer than two years.
    i. Refer to page 19 in this instruction book for information on Adam's employer and his annual salary. (Cabot's telephone number is 937-555-3777.)
    j. For Previous Employer, write N/A because Adam has worked at his current job longer than two years.
    k. For Name of Nearest Relative, list Edward Warner, 22 Sayre Court, Hopewell, OH 45313, 937-555-3935, father.
    l. Under Checking/Savings Account, refer to Illustration 14 for Adam's checking account number. His money market account is also with Hopewell Community Bank, account number 21-909090. (A **money market account** is a type of savings account in which the interest rate changes slightly from time to time. It tends to earn more interest than a regular account.)
    m. The section on Credit Experience shows how much debt (or liabilities) Adam already has. This information is important to the bank. If Adam had significant debt, he might not be able to pay back a car loan. The bank might then turn down his request.

       In the first section, check Rent, write Lakeview Properties under Creditor, and write $900.00 under Monthly Payment. Skip the next two lines because Adam doesn't own property. Under Auto, write 2000 for Year and Meridian SE for Make of Auto. Be sure to write 0 under Balance and Monthly Payment to show that this car is paid for.
    n. The last few lines are for all other debts and credit obligations. List Adam's WorldCard and the account number shown in Illustration 16. List $150.00 as the average monthly payment.
    o. Sign Adam's name and add the date. Adam would give his loan application to Alice, but you should file your copy behind the *Forms* tab in the file folder.

CHECKPOINT

Why is the information about Adam's debt important to the bank?

☐ Activities for March 11

12. Adam and Carson decide to eat dinner at Talia's, an Italian restaurant. Adam pays the $28.60 bill, plus a $5.40 tip, with cash. Record the transaction in the *Financial Record Book* or AGW_FINR file. Write the tip on the receipt (Form 39, page 91) so that you won't forget the amount. Then file the receipt behind the *Receipts* tab in the file folder.

☐ Activities for March 12

13. Adam stops at GasCo for gasoline again. Record the credit card transaction in the *Financial Record Book* or AGW_FINR file, and file the receipt for $34.41 (Form 40, page 91) under *Receipts*.

☐ Activities for March 14

14. Early in the evening, Adam and Carson go shopping for groceries and a few other items. They stop at Fiori's Drug Store, because Carson likes to visit with Mrs. Fiori. Adam pays $24.90 for sundries in cash. Then they go to Hilltop for groceries. The bill there is $70.49, which Adam pays by using his debit card. Record both transactions in the *Financial Record Book* or the AGW_FINR file. In addition, you need to record the second transaction in the checkbook register. File the two receipts (Form 41, page 91 and Form 42, page 93) under *Receipts*.

☐ Activities for March 15

15. Because it looks like it's going to be a rainy day, Adam takes Carson to Children's Museum and Activity Center, where they can see all sorts of exhibits and participate in a variety of activities. The tickets are $18.00, and their lunch is $13.45. Record these two cash payments in the *Financial Record Book* or AGW_FINR file. File the tickets and the receipt (Forms 43 and 44, page 93).

☐ Activities for March 17

16. Because today is the first working day after the 15th, Adam receives another receipt for the direct deposit of his paycheck. Check Form 45 (page 95) to make sure it's accurate before recording the deposit in the *Financial Record Book* or AGW_FINR file and in the checkbook register. File the paycheck receipt under *Receipts*.

17. When Adam picks up Carson at Stay & Play Child Care Center, he writes a check for $620.00 to pay for next month's child care. The payment is due on the 20th of each month. Record the payment in the *Financial Record Book* or AGW_FINR file and in the checkbook register. File the receipt (Form 46, page 95) under *Receipts*.

☐ Activities for March 18

18. At home, Adam goes online to the Web site of Stacks Etc. He owns a software package called BudgetXT, and he wants to learn how to use it to keep track of his finances electronically. He selects a book called *Getting Started with BudgetXT* for $25 and clicks the link labeled Add to My Shopping Cart. That's all he wants to buy, so he clicks Proceed to Checkout. The site sends him to a secure page that shows the amount of his purchase, including shipping, as $29.95. Following instructions at the site, he enters his e-mail address, mailing address, and credit card information. After checking that the information he entered is correct, he clicks Send to complete the transaction. Within minutes, he receives a receipt for his purchase by e-mail. Record the transaction under *Personal* in the *Financial Record Book* or AGW_FINR file. Remember that credit transactions do not get recorded in the checkbook register until Adam pays the credit card bill by check. File the e-mail receipt (Form 47, p. 97) behind the *Receipts* tab.

19. Adam's monthly insurance bill (Form 48, page 99) is due on March 22. He carries three types of insurance with S&T Insurance Company: car, renter's, and life. Adam pays a monthly premium for each of these policies. He bought **renter's insurance** to cover his personal property, such as home furnishings and clothes, in case of loss from fire, theft, or other hazards at his rented townhouse. He carries **life insurance** to provide funds to help care for Carson if Adam were to die while Carson is young.

    To pay the bill, Adam mails a check to S&T Insurance Company for $73.00. Record the check in the checkbook register. In the *Financial Record Book* or AGW_FINR file, record the transaction on one line. However, divide up the total into the appropriate categories for each type of insurance. Refer to Form 48 and Adam's budget worksheet for guidance. File the receipt portion of the bill under *Receipts* and the bill portion under *Checks Written*.

CHECKPOINT

Look at the paycheck receipt Adam receives in the middle of the month (Form 45) and the one he received at the beginning of the month (Form 28). How are the receipts different?

☐ Activities for March 19

20. LaToya, one of the teachers at Stay & Play Child Care, calls Adam to say that Carson has become sick at school. He has a high fever and is complaining that his throat hurts. Before leaving the office, Adam calls Carson's doctor's office to make an appointment.

    Adam picks up Carson and takes him straight to the pediatrician's office. Dr. Washio says Carson has strep throat, and she writes a prescription for medicine.

    Adam belongs to the health insurance plan offered by his employer. It is a network of doctors and health facilities called a **preferred provider organization (PPO)**. The plan will pay most medical expenses as long as Adam goes to doctors within the network. Adam's copayment for the doctor's visit is $25.00. At the drug store, his copayment for the prescription is $20.00, so he pays $20.00 for the medicine. Record two check payments in the *Financial Record Book* or AGW_FINR file and in the checkbook register. File the receipts (Form 49, page 99 and Form 50, page 101).

FYI *If you are using the* **Financial Record Book,** *you will need to total the columns when you get to the bottom of a page. Transfer the totals to the appropriate columns at the top of the next page. Write "Carried Forward" as the description.*

☐ Activities for March 20

21. Because Carson is still not feeling well, Adam must stay home from work to take care of him. While Carson is sleeping, Adam decides to revise his budget to see how much money he can afford for monthly car payments.

    Retrieve his budget worksheet from the file folder, or open AGW_BUDG on the data CD and save it as AGW_BUD2. Make the following revisions to Adam's budget as he finds ways to pull money from other categories to use for a car payment. Make the changes by crossing out the old amounts and writing in the new, or by replacing the figures in the spreadsheet cells in the AGW_BUD2 file.

    a. Adam lowers his clothes and shoes limit to $275.00.
    b. The new car shouldn't require as much maintenance, so he lowers that limit to $35.00.
    c. Adam decides that he and Carson can eat out less often and at less expensive restaurants, so he lowers that amount to $120.00.

✔ Math Check

Total the amount of money Adam is pulling from clothing and shoes, car maintenance, and restaurant meals. How much does Adam have for a monthly car payment so far? He pulled $125 from the clothing budget, $50 from car maintenance, and $30 from restaurant meals. At this point, he has $205 to put toward a monthly car payment.

    d. Adam realizes his car insurance premium might go up for a new car, so he calls his insurance agent, Mary Baker. Mary estimates that his insurance premium will be about $75.00 monthly. This payment will require $30.00 more than he's spending now for insurance, so subtract that amount from your sum above. Now how much does Adam have to work with? Your answer should be $175.

    Adam isn't sure how much his new car will cost, but he guesses that $175.00 a month will not be enough for a good new car, so he returns to his budget to make more changes.

    e. As much as Adam enjoys movies and sports, he decides to switch to a different cable package that includes fewer channels. The new package will cost $70. The switch will save him $20 a month.
    f. Next, Adam reduces his budget for event fees and tickets to $50.00.
    g. Finally, he subtracts $25 from his allotment for gifts.

✔ Math Check

How much does Adam have for a car payment now? You should have arrived at $230.00.

h. Enter $230.00 for Car Loan Payment under Transportation on the budget worksheet or file. Total the revised amounts in all budget categories to check that it still equals his net pay for the month.

22. Adam knows that one way he can keep his monthly car payments low is by paying as much as possible up front. The less money he borrows, the lower his payments will be. Adam decides to figure out how much money he can use for his **down payment** on the car.

    Retrieve Adam's net worth form from the file folder, or open AGW_NETW, to review his assets.

    a. First, Adam will trade in his old car. He went online to the Kelley Blue Book Web site. After entering information about his car's model, year, mileage, features, and condition, he found that it is worth about $1,700.00.
    b. Adam briefly considers taking money from his 401(k) retirement account but decides it's better to leave that money alone. The financial penalty for withdrawing the money early would take a big bite out of his retirement savings.
    c. Finally, Adam looks at his savings account that he's been using to save money for a new car or other major purchase. He decides to leave some money in this account for emergencies, but he's willing to withdraw $3,600.00 for the down payment.

✔ Math Check

How much does Adam have for a down payment? You should have arrived at $5,300.00.

Now that Adam knows how much he has for a down payment and how much he can afford for monthly car payments, he can start shopping for a new car. In the meantime, he'll wait to hear whether his bank will approve a loan for him or whether he'll have to get a loan through the car dealership.

CHECKPOINT

Where does Adam plan to get the $5,300 down payment for buying a car? How much will he get from each source?

☐ Activities for March 21

23. Carson is already feeling better, so Adam takes him to school and heads for the office. On the way, he stops for gasoline, once again using his credit card to pay the $33.85. Record the transaction in the *Financial Record Book* or AGW_FINR file, and file the receipt (Form 51, page 101).

☐ Activities for March 22

24. Adam and Carson do their weekly grocery shopping. As usual, Adam uses his debit card to pay for the $92.14 in food and other items. Record the transaction in both records and file the receipt (Form 52, page 101).
25. Adam and Carson stop at the video store and pick out some movies to rent. Adam pays the $14.98 rental fee in cash. He doesn't get a receipt, but he remembers to record the transaction when he gets home. Record the cash payment.

☐ Activities for March 23

26. Despite Adam's big purchase coming up in the near future, he must buy some new clothes for himself and for Carson. He writes a check for $222.60 to pay for a blazer from Delker Clothing. He also writes a check for $28.45 for Carson's new shoes from Shamrock Shoes. Finally, he writes a check to Park Department Stores for $64.46 for some new clothes for Carson. Record the transactions in both records and file the receipts (Forms 53, 54, and 55 on page 103).

☐ Activities for March 25

27. Alice Littlebear, from Hopewell Community Bank, called yesterday to say that Adam's loan has been approved if he wants to use it.

With this approval, he can start looking at cars tonight. But first, he and Carson stop at Burger Express for a quick dinner. Record his cash payment of $9.82 in the *Financial Record Book* or AGW_FINR file, and file the receipt (Form 56, page 103).

After dinner, Adam and Carson stop at two car dealerships, one for new cars and one for used cars. At both places, the salespeople tell him that with a down payment of $5,300.00 and a five-year loan with monthly payments of $230.00 or less, he should be looking at cars in the $14,000 to $16,000 range. Adam decides his next step should be a trip to the library and the Internet to research new and almost-new cars in that price range.

☐ Activities for March 26

28. Adam receives his credit card bill from World-Card. To keep his debt under control, he pays the entire balance on his credit card each month. Retrieve the three gas receipts and the receipt for his online purchase. Use them to make sure the bill is correct. If it is, write the total amount on the line next to *Payment Enclosed*. Then record a check for $133.45 in the checkbook register only. Because this payment represents credit transactions that have already been recorded in the *Financial Record Book* or AGW_FINR file, do not deduct this amount there again. File the two portions of the bill (Form 57, page 105) behind the appropriate tabs in the file folder.

☐ Activities for March 27

29. Adam fills his car's gas tank at GasCo and charges the $33.27 to his credit card. Record the credit card payment and file the receipt (Form 58, page 107).

30. Adam stops for groceries at Hilltop. His total is $87.14, which he pays with his debit card. Record the transaction and file the receipt (Form 59, page 107).

☐ Activities for March 28

31. Because of all the planning, research, and shopping he is doing, Adam feels ready to buy a new car tomorrow. He would like to be prepared to buy a car as soon as he finds one that meets his requirements. So, he transfers $3,600.00 from his savings account into his checking account. Record this deposit in the *Financial Record Book* or AGW_FINR file and in the checkbook register.

CHECKPOINT

What is Adam's savings account balance after he transfers money to his checking account?

☐ Activities for March 29

32. This past week Adam went to the library to check out car-buying guides. He also spent several hours researching cars online. He read reviews of different models at car-oriented Web sites. At one site he compared prices and features of different models (Illustration 19). He also asked several friends and relatives for advice. He has narrowed his choices to three car models. He's decided to buy a used car if it is one of those three models, is no more than two years old, and has been driven less than 20,000 miles.

    Adam's parents have agreed to watch Carson for the day, so Adam heads for the car dealerships. By about 3:00 in the afternoon, he's decided which of the three types of car he wants, so he goes back to that dealership. They have two used cars that fit all his requirements. He decides to go with the one that is slightly more expensive but has been driven fewer miles. He and the car sales representative, Bob Chen, negotiate a fair price for the car. Bob explains the loan options offered by the dealership, but Adam decides to use the loan from his own bank. It has the lowest interest rate. **Interest** is the fee for using borrowed money.

    Record a check for $3,600.00 to Trent County Auto Mall in the *Financial Record Book* or AGW_FINR file and in the checkbook register. File the receipt (Form 60, page 109).

Illustration 19:
Online Vehicle Comparison

VEHICLE COMPARISON

Pricing | Features | Specs

PRICING

Pricing	Breeze Sedan	Red Hawk LT Sedan	Olympic S Sedan
Retail	$14,220	$15,292	$14,770
Invoice	$13,532	$14,276	$13,431
Destination Charge	$545	$575	$485
Warranty			
Basic	3 yr./36000 mi.	4 yr./50000 mi.	3 yr./36000 mi.
Drivetrain	5 yr./100000 mi.	5 yr./60000 mi.	5 yr./60000 mi.
Rust	5 yr./Unlimited mi.	12 yr./Unlimited mi.	5 yr./Unlimited mi.

FEATURES

Base Engine Type & Cylinders	Inline 4	Inline 4	Inline 4
Base Engine Displacement	2.0 liters	2.0 liters	1.8 liters
Valvetrain	16 Valves double overhead cam (DOHC)	8 Valves single overhead cam (SOHC)	16 Valves double overhead cam (DOHC)
Horsepower	130 hp @ 5300 rpm	115 hp @ 5200 rpm	130 hp @ 6000 rpm
Torque	135 ft-lbs.@ 4500 rpm	122 ft-lbs. @ 2600 rpm	125 ft-lbs.@ 4200 rpm
4 Cyl	Standard	Standard	Standard
4 Speed Automatic	Optional	Not Available	Not Available
5 Speed Manual	Standard	Standard	Standard
Driven Wheels	Front wheel drive	Front wheel drive	Front wheel drive
Independent Suspension	Four-wheel	Four-wheel	Front
Stabilizer Bars	Front and rear	Front and rear	Front and rear
Tires	All season	All season	All season
Wheels	Alloy rims 16 in.	Steel rims 15 x 6 in.	Steel rims 16 x 6.5 in.
Spare	Spacesaver	Fullsize	Spacesaver
Front Wipers	Intermittent	Variable intermittent	Intermittent
Rear Wipers	Rear window wiper	Intermittent rear wiper	Intermittent rear wiper—optional
Rear Defogger	Standard	Standard	Standard
Privacy Glass	Standard	Not available	Not available
Total Seating Capacity	5	5	5
Front Seat Type	Sport	Bucket	Bucket
Upholstery Type	Premium cloth	Cloth	Cloth

☐ Activities for March 31

33. After he picks up Carson from daycare, they stop at a bookstore to pick up a birthday present for one of Carson's friends and to let Carson get a new book for himself. Carson chooses a book about dinosaurs for his friend. He picks out a book about a family of bears for himself. Adam writes a check to Bit-Zee Booksellers for $18.55. Record the payment in the *Financial Record Book* or AGW_FINR file and in the checkbook register. File the receipt (Form 61, page 109).

34. Later in the evening, Adam reconciles his checkbook. Unlike Tyra's bank, Adam's bank does not return the cancelled checks. Instead, Hopewell Community Bank sends just a statement (Form 62, pages 111–112). Notice that this statement was prepared on 3/27, so any deposits made or checks cashed after that date will not be shown on this form. As you learned in Part 2, *outstanding checks* are checks that have not yet finished their route through the banking system. As a result, Adam's bank has not yet subtracted the amounts from his checking account. Outstanding checks are one reason why the ending balance on your statement often doesn't agree with the ending balance in your checkbook register. To make sure your records and the bank's records are correct, then, you must reconcile the two.

    Follow these steps to reconcile Adam's checkbook:

    a. Compare all checks, deposits, online bill payments, and debit card transactions shown on the statement against the checkbook register. Check off each one that's correct. Like most banks, Hopewell lists the dates it paid the checks, not the dates the checks were written. The register should show one deposit and three outstanding checks that aren't shown on the statement.
    b. To reconcile an account when the balance on the statement does not match the balance in the checkbook register, follow these steps on the back of the statement: On line 1, enter the closing balance shown on the bank statement.
    c. In the spaces provided in part 2, record the deposit Adam made after the statement was prepared. Record the deposit total in the blank for line 2.
    d. Add the amounts in lines 1 and 2, and enter this subtotal in line 3.
    e. In the spaces provided in part 4, list the three outstanding checks. Then add the amounts of the checks and enter the total in the blank for line 4.
    f. Subtract line 4 from line 3, and enter this revised bank balance in line 5.
    g. In line 6, enter the balance shown in the checkbook register. Next, enter the service charge and the interest shown on the bank statement. Follow the instructions in line 6 for adding and subtracting amounts, and enter the result in the blank for line 6.

✔ Math Check

The amounts on lines 5 and 6 should match. This is the true amount of money currently in the account: $1,138.40. If the amounts do not match, follow the advice at the bottom of the reconciliation form for checking your work.

    h. The bank automatically withdraws a monthly fee of $10.00 from Adam's checking account for the online bill payment service. Record this service charge in the checkbook register. Record it under *Miscellaneous* in the *Financial Record Book*.
    i. The bank pays Adam interest for keeping his money in their bank. Record the interest shown on the statement, $1.26, as a deposit in the checkbook register and in the *Financial Record Book*. The checkbook register should now show a balance of $1,138.40, the same ending balance shown on the reconciliation form.

✔ Math Check

Before proving cash in the Financial Record Book or AGW_FINR file, reconstruct Adam's cash transactions to determine how much cash he has left. Did you discover $64.85 in Adam's wallet?

On a separate piece of paper, add the amount of Adam's remaining cash to the ending balance in Adam's checkbook register. You may think that this total should match the ending balance in your *Financial Record Book* or AGW_FINR file, as it did in Tyra's case. But it doesn't match. In fact, this balance should be $33.27 higher than the balance in the *Financial Record Book.* Can you figure out why?

It's because Adam charged $33.27 for gasoline to his credit card, which has already been deducted from the balance in the *Financial Record Book.* However, he hasn't paid the credit card company yet, so the amount hasn't been deducted from his checking account balance. This fact explains the difference in the two balances.

35. As the last step, total each of the payment columns (both pages) in the *Financial Record Book* or AGW_FINR file. Write your answers in the boxes at the bottom of each column on the second page.

CHECKPOINT

If you have outstanding checks when your bank statement is produced, will your bank statement balance be greater than or less than the current balance in your checkbook register. Why?

Jump$tart Coalition for Personal Financial Literacy

National Standards in K-12 Personal Finance Education

Planning and Money Management

Standard 4: Apply consumer skills to purchase decisions.

You might not be planning to make a major purchase in the next few months, but you can learn a lot about purchase decisions from Adam's car-buying experience. Planning, research, and shopping around can help you make good decisions for all kinds of purchases.

Activities

1. Think about some of your routine purchases. Describe an example of how planning, research, and shopping could help you make better buying decisions.
2. Ask a family member how they made their most recent major purchase decision. Summarize your discussion.

Special Topics

Locate the following Special Topic readings on the Data CD. Read the article and answer the Think It Through questions that appear at the end of the article.

- Special Topic 7: Good Debt vs. Bad Debt
- Special Topic 8: Research Before You Buy
- Special Topic 9: Share the Wealth: Time, Treasure, and Talent

Part 4 Investing in the Future

Performance Outcomes

In the last phase of this simulation, you will learn to:

1. Prepare a statement of net worth and a budget for a married couple.
2. Estimate federal income taxes for a self-employed person.
3. Find a reliable financial planner.
4. Investigate various ways to use your money to earn money.
5. Understand the purpose of different kinds of insurance.
6. Fill out a home loan qualifying application.
7. Continue developing sound financial practices involving recordkeeping, decision making, and planning.

© Getty Images, Trinette Reed, Digital Vision

Meet Celina and Jared Hoffman

Thirty-two-year-old Celina Hoffman has been married to Jared Hoffman, also 32, for eight years. Shortly after marrying, they bought a small house. Their address is 363 Sherwood Circle, Maplewood, OH 44922. Their home telephone number is (419) 555-4576. The Hoffmans also have two cell phones. Jared's number is (419) 555-9178 and Celina's is (419) 555-9113.

Jared is a registered nurse. He has worked at the Maplewood Medical Center for six years. His Social Security number is 912-65-0018. His annual salary is $54,000. About three years ago, Celina started her own business, Maplewood PC Services. Celina installs and repairs personal computers in homes and small businesses. She enjoys working for herself, but she works very hard and puts in many hours to make the business a success. She estimates that she will earn about

$42,000 this year. Her Social Security number is 076-45-5013.

Celina and Jared would like to buy a larger house. Lately, they've been thinking that in addition to purchasing a new home, they should begin saving for retirement. They will need to find ways to meet these financial goals. Although they've budgeted for expenses and savings since they were married, they want to use the money they are earning more wisely. They need both a short-term plan and a long-term plan for how to use their money in the future.

Figuring Out the Hoffmans' Net Worth

Determine Celina and Jared's net worth by retrieving Form 63 (page 113 of this instruction book) or by calling up the NETWORTH_4 file on the data disk. Refer to the directions on page 3 in this instruction book if needed.

Use the information shown here to complete the Hoffmans' net worth form. File the completed Form 26 behind the *Forms* tab of the file folder, or save your document as CJH_NETW.

Assets

- $6,922.82 in a checking account.
- $11,140.21 in a savings account.
- $8,800.00 in certificates of deposit.
- Current value of their house, $125,000.
- Current value of their two cars, $17,100.00.
- Value of their personal items, $7,500.
- $265 in cash.

Liabilities

- Mortgage, $95,200.00
- Universal Cellular phone bill, $87.45
- Tri-County Gas & Electric bill, $112.28.
- Pilot Internet Connections payment due, $41.95
- TDS Satellite TV bill, $54.99
- Car loans, $11,946.00.
- Homeowner's insurance, $47.50.
- Annual car registration fee (for Celina), $55.00.
- Income tax (for Celina), $2,770.00.
- Property tax, $1,650.00.

✔ Math Check

Be sure to check your math before filing Form 63 in the *Forms* section or saving this file as CJH_NETW.

Writing Out the Hoffmans' Budget

Begin by retrieving Form 64 (page 113 in this instruction book) or calling up BUDGET from the data CD. Use the figures that appear on the next page to fill out the Hoffmans' worksheet. The figures are rounded to the nearest dollar.

File the Hoffmans' budget worksheet under Forms or save the document as CJH_BUDG.

Once again, you will work through one month's worth of financial transactions. Check the box as you complete each day's activities.

✔ Math Check

Total your entries in all categories to make sure your sum matches the Hoffmans' combined monthly net pay.

THE HOFFMANS' BUDGET INFORMATION

Monthly Income
Gross Pay, $8,000
Taxes/Deductions, $1,288
Net Pay, $6,712

Savings/Debt Payoff
Savings Accounts, $2,090.00

Home
Mortgage Payment, $830.00
Property Tax, $275.00
Utilities, $175.00
Cell Phone Service, $90.00
Satellite TV Service, $55.00
Internet Service, $42.00
Home Maintenance, $60.00
Homeowner's Insurance, $48.00

Food/Sundries
Food, $280.00
Personal Care Items, $90.00
Small Home Care Items, $45.00

Personal
Clothes and Shoes, $375.00
Haircuts/Salon Services, $100.00
Dry Cleaning/Laundry, $25.00

Transportation
Car Loan Payments, $460.00
Car Insurance, $240.00
Gasoline/Oil, $250
Car Maintenance, $120.00
License/Registration Fees, $10.00

Entertainment
Restaurant Meals, $400.00
Event Fees/Tickets, $90.00
Travel Expenses, $350.00

Miscellaneous
Gifts, $125.00
Bank Service Charges, $7.00

Health Care
Doctor and Dental Fees, $35.00
Prescription Medicines, $20.00
Glasses/Contact Lenses, $25.00

April Transactions

☐ Activities for April 1

1. On the first page of the *Financial Record Book* for Phase 3, enter the Hoffmans' total amount of spendable money (checking account balance plus cash shown on their net worth statement). Enter the date as 4/1, record the description as Opening Balance, and enter the amount in the *Balance* column. Or, open FINREC on your data CD, record the opening balance, and save the document as CJH_FINR.

   Start a new page in the checkbook register and enter the Hoffmans' checking account balance in the first Balance Fwd box.

2. Jared makes a mortgage payment on the first of each month. A **mortgage** is a home loan. The payment is due on the eighth day of the month and Jared wants to make sure the check arrives on time or early. He doesn't want their credit rating damaged by late payments. Just as you did in Part 3, you will record all checking account transactions in the *Financial Record Book* and checkbook register, without actually writing checks or deposit tickets. Record a payment of $830.00 to Lancaster State Bank in the *Financial Record Book* or CJH_FINR file and in the checkbook register (check #1312). File the mortgage payment receipt (Form 65, page 115) under *Checks Written*.

☐ Activities for April 2

3. On his way home from work, Jared stops at Capital Service Station to put gasoline in his car. He uses his debit card to pay for the gas. Record a debit card payment of $35.25 in the *Financial Record Book* or CJH_FINR file and in the checkbook register. File the receipt (Form 66, page 115) under *Receipts*.
4. Next, Jared stops at Family Foods for grocery shopping. Record another debit card payment of $97.94 in the *Financial Record Book* or CJH_FINR file and in the checkbook register. File the receipt (Form 67, page 115) under *Receipts*.

☐ Activities for April 3

5. One of Celina's neighbors is retiring soon, so Celina stops at a shop called Regalo to buy a gift. Record a check for $36.57 in the *Financial Record Book* or CJH_FINR file and in the checkbook register. File the receipt (Form 68, page 117) under *Receipts*.

☐ Activities for April 4

6. Celina and Jared invite Celina's parents to dinner at Water Point Grille. As they're enjoying their meal, Jared mentions that he and Celina are seriously thinking of moving to a bigger house. Celina's father points out that buying a house generally is a good investment, but he suggests that Celina and Jared look into other types of investments. Celina's mother also suggests that the couple find a professional financial planner who can help them plan the best ways to spend and invest their money.

   Record a cash payment of $108.12 plus a tip of $21.88 in the *Financial Record Book* or CJH_FINR file. Write the amount of the tip on the receipt (Form 69, page 117) and file the receipt.

☐ Activities for April 5

7. Because Celina works for herself she has to handle her income taxes in a special way. **Self-employed** people are required to estimate their income for the current year and figure the income tax they would owe on this income. Then they make partial payments on the tax four times a year (quarterly), starting April 15. Because this deadline is coming soon, Celina figures her estimated tax for the year so that she'll know how much tax to pay now.

   Begin by removing Form 70 from page 119. Form 1040-ES is used to figure estimated taxes. Celina will be filing with the IRS as a married person filing separately. This means she and Jared will each file a separate tax form because Celina's income tax payments are made quarterly and Jared's are made through payroll deductions throughout the year.

   a. Celina estimates that her adjusted gross income (income + taxable interest from savings) will be $42,175.00. Enter this amount on line 1.
   b. Celina decides to use the standard deduction, which is $5,450.00 for a married person filing separately. Enter this amount on line 2.
   c. Follow the directions for line 3.
   d. Celina takes only one exemption. Look at the information on the form and enter the appropriate amount on line 4.
   e. Follow the directions for line 5 to find Celina's taxable income.
   f. Using the tax chart (Illustration 20), find Celina's income on Schedule Y-2 and follow the directions for calculating the income tax amount. This amount is determined by adding $4,481 plus the 25% of the amount on line 5 that is over $32,550. Here are the calculations:

      $\$33{,}225 - \$32{,}550 = \$675$

      $\$672 \times 0.25 = \$168.75$

      $\$168.75 + 4{,}481.25 = \$4{,}650.00$

   Enter $4,650.00 on line 6.

Illustration 20: Estimated Income Tax Chart

20_ _ Tax Rate Schedules

Caution. *Do not use these Tax Rate Schedules to figure your 20_ _ taxes. Use only to figure your 20_ _ estimated taxes.*

Schedule X—Use if your 20_ _ filing status is Single

If line 5 is: Over—	But not over—	The tax is:	of the amount over—
$0	$8,025	------------ 10%	$0
8,025	32,550	$802.50 + 15%	8,025
32,550	78,850	4,481.25 + 25%	32,550
78,850	164,550	16,056.25 + 28%	78,850
164,550	357,700	40,052.25 + 33%	164,550
357,700	------------	103,791.75 + 35%	357,700

Schedule Z—Use if your 20_ _ filing status is Head of household

If line 5 is: Over—	But not over—	The tax is:	of the amount over—
$0	$11,450	------------ 10%	$0
11,450	43,650	$1,145.00 + 15%	11,450
43,650	112,650	5,975.00 + 25%	43,650
112,650	182,400	23,225.00 + 28%	112,650
182,400	357,700	42,755.00 + 33%	182,400
357,700	------------	100,604.00 + 35%	357,700

Schedule Y-1—Use if your 20_ _ filing status is Married filing jointly or Qualifying widow(er)

If line 5 is: Over—	But not over—	The tax is:	of the amount over—
$0	$16,050	------------ 10%	$0
16,050	65,100	$1,605.00 + 15%	16,050
65,100	131,450	8,962.50 + 25%	65,100
131,450	200,300	25,550.00 + 28%	131,450
200,300	357,700	44,828.00 + 33%	200,300
357,700	------------	96,770.00 + 35%	357,700

Schedule Y-2—Use if your 20_ _ filing status is Married filing separately

If line 5 is: Over—	But not over—	The tax is:	of the amount over—
$0	$8,025	------------ 10%	$0
8,025	32,550	$802.50 + 15%	8,025
32,550	65,725	4,481.25 + 25%	32,550
65,725	100,150	12,775.00 + 28%	65,725
100,150	178,850	22,414.00 + 33%	100,150
178,850	------------	48,385.00 + 35%	178,850

g. Because line 7 doesn't apply to Celina, record 0 on line 7 and transfer the amount from line 6 to line 8.

h. Line 9 also doesn't apply to Celina. Record 0 on line 9 and follow the instructions for line 10.

i. In the blank space within the line 11 instructions, record the amount Celina expects to earn this year: $42,000. Because this amount is less than $102,000, multiply her earnings from self-employment, $42,000, by 15.3%. (Note that interest income is not included.) Enter the result on line 11.

j. Because there are no other taxes, record 0 on line 12. Add lines 10 and 11 and enter the sum on line 13a.

k. Celina does not qualify for the earned income credit or additional child tax credit, so record 0 on line 13b. Transfer the amount from line 13a to line 13c.

l. Follow the directions for line 14a.

m. Celina's income tax for last year was $10,810.00. Enter that amount on line 14b.

n. Follow the directions for line 14c and record the appropriate amount. This amount is the total estimated tax Celina will pay on her income for this year. She must divide this total by four and pay it in quarterly amounts called **installments**. At the end of the year she will figure the actual tax she owes when she fills out her tax return. At that time she will pay any additional tax she owes or will receive a tax refund if she paid too much in estimated installments.

o. Because Celina does not have taxes withheld, record 0 on line 15.

p. Follow the directions for 16a and 16b. Your answers for both questions should be *No*.

q. Follow the directions for line 17 to find out how much tax Celina should pay in each installment. When the installment amount has cents, you are allowed to round the amount to the nearest dollar.

✔ Math Check

Make sure you have the correct answers for these three lines: line 11, $6,426.00; line 13c, $11,076.00; and line 14c, $9,968.40.

Celina's final step is to write a check to the United States Treasury for her first installment. She mails the check, along with a special form called a **payment voucher** (Illustration 21), to the Internal Revenue Service (IRS). Record a check for $2,492.00 to the United States Treasury in the *Financial Record Book* or CJH_FINR file under Savings/Debt Payoff and in the checkbook register. File Form 70 (Form 1040-ES) under *Forms*. Note that Celina will have to make a payment of $2,492.00 every three months. Therefore, she should establish a habit of setting aside a third of this total each month ($830.67) under Savings/Debt Payoff to save for the rest of the income tax installments this year.

CHECKPOINT

Why does Celina pay quarterly taxes and Jared does not?

☐ Activities for April 7

8. Celina and Jared plan to spend a day working in the yard. They want their house to look nice, especially if they're going to sell it. So, they go to Sumida's, a lawn and garden shop, where Mr. Sumida helps them pick out the things they need. Record a check for $72.48 in the *Financial Record Book* or CJH_FINR file and in the checkbook register. File the receipt (Form 71, page 121).
9. On the way back to their house, Jared and Celina stop to pick up coffee and a cinnamon roll. They do not get a receipt, but Jared writes the amount, $5.39, on the receipts from the garden store. Record the cash transaction in the *Financial Record Book* or CJH_FINR file.

☐ Activities for April 8

10. Celina and Jared go to Family Foods for more groceries. Record a debit card payment for $72.32 in the *Financial Record Book* or CJH_FINR file and in the checkbook register. File the receipt (Form 72, page 121).

☐ Activities for April 9

11. It's time for Jared to pay some bills. He goes to his bank's Web site and enters his user ID and PIN to log in. He then clicks the links to the bill payment page. Jared enters the following payments: Universal Cellular, $87.40; Tri-County Gas & Electric, $112.28; and TDS Satellite TV, $49.82. Record these online payments in the *Financial Record Book* or CJH_FINR file and in the checkbook register. File the receipt portions of the bills (Forms 73, 74, and 75, pages 123-127) under *Receipts* and the bill portions under *Checks Written*.

Illustration 21: Payment Voucher for First Estimated Tax Installment

Form **1040-ES**
Department of the Treasury
Internal Revenue Service

20__ Estimated Tax

Payment Voucher 1 OMB No. 1545-0074

Calendar year—Due April 15, 20__

File only if you are making a payment of estimated tax by check or money order. Mail this voucher with your check or money order payable to the **"United States Treasury."** Write your social security number and "20__ Form 1040-ES" on your check or money order. Do not send cash. Enclose, but do not staple or attach, your payment with this voucher.

Amount of estimated tax you are paying by check or money order.

Dollars	Cents
2,492	00

Print or type

Your first name and initial	Your last name	Your social security number
Celina	Hoffman	076-45-5031

If joint payment, complete for spouse

Spouse's first name and initial	Spouse's last name	Spouse's social security number

Address (number, street, and apt. no.)
363 Sherwood Circle

City, state, and ZIP code. (If a foreign address, enter city, province or state, postal code, and country.)
Maplewood, OH 44922

☐ Activities for April 10

12. Celina and Jared think that finding a financial planner is a good idea. Although they could research their investment options on their own, they know it would use up much of their free time. Also, they would prefer to have an expert's opinion. So for the past several days, they've been visiting Web sites of financial magazines, banks, investment companies, and consumer organizations to learn more about financial planning and investing. They've also been checking the telephone book and online for names of financial planners and asking friends for recommendations. They've discovered they have many choices.

    Several local banks and investment companies have **certified financial planners** on staff. These investment professionals are trained to help clients achieve their financial goals through sound planning and investing. Some financial planners are paid on commission. This means that they receive a small portion of the profits your investments earn. Other financial planners charge a flat fee for each hour of financial review and advice. Celina and Jared have decided to work with Delores Cruz-Smith, who charges a flat fee of $130.00 an hour.

    First, Delores looks over the Hoffmans' statement of net worth, their monthly budget, and their financial record. Next, she asks them to define their goals. They tell her that their goals are to buy a larger house soon and to save for retirement. Delores asks the couple many detailed questions about these goals and then makes several recommendations:

    a. **Pay off the car loans.** The Hoffmans have two car loans, both of which have rather high interest rates, near 10%. Paying off the loans sooner will save them money because they won't have to pay as much interest.

    b. **Contribute to a 401(k) or an IRA.** Delores says that saving even a little more each month will make a big difference in the total at retirement. To make her point, she shows them a chart of the total savings with 401(k) contributions of 6% of salary compared to 3% (Illustration 22). Jared can participate in his employer's 401(k) plan. Because Celina's business has no retirement plan, she can set up an **individual retirement account (IRA)**. Not only are retirement accounts a great way to invest and earn interest, but they also provide a "tax break." Money put into either a 401(k) or a traditional IRA is **tax-deferred income**. Jared and Celina wouldn't have to pay income tax now on money deposited into such accounts. The taxes are put off, or "deferred," until the funds are withdrawn at retirement age. A **Roth IRA** offers a different kind of tax break. Jared and Celina would have to pay taxes on the income they contribute now, but they wouldn't pay taxes when they withdraw the money. This means that the earnings on the Roth IRA funds are never taxed.

    c. **Purchase a term life insurance policy on Celina.** Jared already has life insurance as a **fringe benefit** of his job. But if Celina died suddenly, Jared would have a difficult time meeting his financial obligations

Illustration 22:
401(k) Earnings Potential Chart

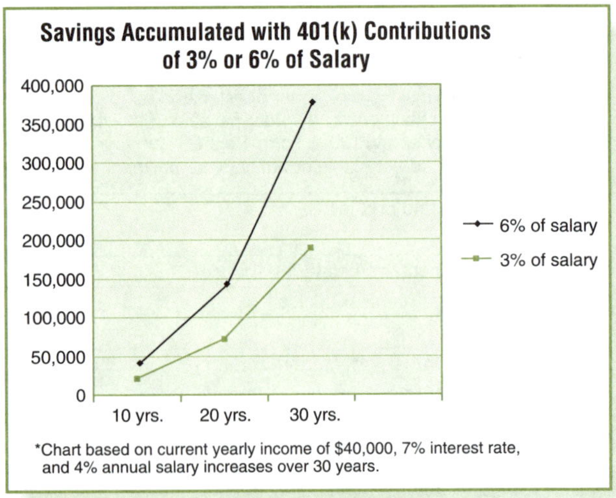

without her income. Delores recommends buying a **term life insurance** policy that would pay Jared $500,000.00 if Celina died within the 20-year time period, or "term," that the policy is in force.

d. **Invest in mutual funds.** Although Delores approves of keeping a sizable amount in savings for emergencies, she also thinks that the extra income the Hoffmans earn in the future should be invested in mutual funds. She explains that mutual funds **diversify** or spread the risk among the stocks and bonds of many organizations. If the Hoffmans bought stock in just a few individual companies, their entire investment would depend on the performance of those few companies. With mutual funds, the collection is so large that if some of the stocks lose value, others will likely gain value, offsetting the losses.

e. **Buy a new home.** One good reason for Celina and Jared to buy a new house is that interest rates on mortgages are lower now than they were when they bought their current house. Thus, they could get a slightly more expensive house by borrowing money at a lower interest rate and still make about the same monthly payments as they do now.

   An alternative to moving to a new house would be to **refinance** their current mortgage. This means they would take out a new mortgage at a lower interest rate to pay off the current high-interest mortgage. Refinancing can require large fees, so the Hoffmans would have to make sure the interest rate would be low enough to make paying the fees worthwhile.

At the end of the meeting, Jared and Celina pay Delores for three hours of her time. Record a check for $390.00 to Delores Cruz-Smith in the Financial Record Book or CJH_FINR file under Miscellaneous and in the checkbook register. File the receipt (Form 76, page 129).

CHECKPOINT

What are the two common methods of paying for financial planning services?

☐ Activities for April 11

13. Jared and Celina stop at Capital Service for gasoline. Record a debit card payment of $34.11 in the *Financial Record Book* or CJH_FINR file and in the checkbook register. File the receipt (Form 77, page 129).
14. Celina's car registration fee is due. Record a check for $55.00 to the Ohio Department of Motor Vehicles in the *Financial Record Book* or CJH_FINR file and in the checkbook register. File the receipt portion of Form 78 (page 131) under *Receipts,* and file the out-going portion under *Checks Written.*

☐ Activities for April 13

15. Based on the financial planner's advice, the Hoffmans have decided to take advantage of the 401(k) plan offered by Jared's employer. Maplewood Medical Center's 401(k) plan limits employee contributions to 10% of their pay. For the first 5%, the employer will contribute 50 cents for each dollar the employee contributes. Jared decides to put in 5% of his pay to maximize his employer's contribution.

    To see how Jared enrolls in the 401(k) plan, retrieve Form 79 from page 133. Follow along as Celina and Jared fill out this form.

    a. Use the following information to complete the top portion. Name: Jared Hoffman. Social Security number: 912-65-0018. Date of Birth: 1/8/19--. Marital status: married.
    b. For item 1, circle 5%.
    c. For item 2, Celina and Jared must decide how to divide the money they contribute to the 401(k) account among these six investment options. The options are ranked in order of risk. The first option has the lowest risk and will likely earn the lowest interest. The last option has the most risk but also the highest earning potential. Because they want to increase

their assets and they're young enough to afford to take some risks, they decide to put 10% in option 3, 30% in option 4, 40% in option 5, and 20% in option 6. Write these percentages on the appropriate lines. Their choices should total 100%.

d. Jared designates Celina as the single primary beneficiary. He lists his parents, who are divorced, as the secondary beneficiaries. For item 3, fill in the following information: 100%, Celina Hoffman, spouse. For item 4, fill in the following information: 50%, Vera Clark, mother; 50% Kirby Hoffman, father.

e. Jared signs and dates the form and gives it to the employee benefits specialist at the hospital. The specialist says the contributions will begin with the next pay period. File the form in the file folder.

FYI *In addition to a 401(k) enrollment form, many employers provide enrollment packets that contain details about investment options. Some employers use the company web site to share this information with employees.*

☐ Activities for April 14

16. After dropping off some clothing at the dry cleaner, Celina stops at Family Foods for groceries. Record a debit card payment of $84.71 in the *Financial Record Book* or CJH_FINR file and in the checkbook register. File the receipt (Form 80, page 135).

17. At home, Celina checks her e-mail and finds a receipt from Pilot Internet Connections. Last month at Pilot's Web site, she signed up for the **automatic bill payment** program. To get started, she filled out an online form that included her name, address, phone number, e-mail address, and credit card number. Now, Pilot automatically charges the monthly Internet connection fee to her WorldCard and sends her an e-mail receipt of the transaction. Record the $41.34 credit card transaction in the *Financial Record Book* or CJH_FINR file. (Remember that charge payments aren't recorded in the checkbook register until the credit card bill is paid.) File the e-mail receipt (Form 81, page 135) under *Receipts*.

☐ Activities for April 15

18. Celina goes online to compare prices for $500,000, 20-year term life insurance policies. She fills out online applications for quotations from five insurance companies. **Quotations** are written descriptions of the terms and prices of the policies offered. Before choosing a company, Celina goes to the library to check the company's rating in *Best's Insurance Reports,* published by the A.M. Best Company. She wants to make sure the insurance company has a good track record for paying **claims**. Celina talks it over with Jared and they decide to buy a policy from Linwood Pace Life Insurance Company. The **premiums** (payments) will be $420.00 each year for the next 20 years. Record a check for $420.00 in the *Financial Record Book* or CJH_FINR file under Personal and in the checkbook register.

19. Record the direct deposit of Jared's paycheck for $1,606.09 in the *Financial Record Book* or CJH_FINR file and in the checkbook register. (Assume that Jared received a paycheck receipt for this direct deposit.)

☐ Activities for April 16

20. Celina and Jared are planning to paint their kitchen next weekend, so they go to Goldberg's Hardware for paint and brushes. Record a check for $86.09 in the *Financial Record Book* or CJH_FINR file and in the checkbook register. File the receipt (Form 82, page 137).

21. Celina and Jared have **homeowner's insurance**. It will help pay for replacing stolen possessions or repairing damage to their house caused by fire, storms, or other hazards. Record a check for $47.50 to PaxCo Insurance Co. in the *Financial Record Book* or CJH_FINR file and in the checkbook register. File the two portions of Form 83 (page 137) in the appropriate places.

☐ Activities for April 18

22. Jared needs some clothes for work. Comfort First Uniforms is having a sale, so he buys three sets of scrubs. Record a check for $72.04 in the *Financial Record Book* or CJH_FINR file and in the checkbook register. File the receipt (Form 84, page 139).

☐ Activities for April 19

23. Jared's sister Rania calls to invite Celina and Jared to join her and her friend Kyle for dinner and a play on April 24. Rania and Kyle already have their tickets. After making sure Jared wants to go to the play, Celina calls the theater box office and uses her WorldCard credit card to purchase two tickets. Record a payment of $75.00 to the Hopewell Playhouse in the *Financial Record Book* or CJH_FINR file. Do not record it in the checkbook register until the credit card bill is paid. When Celina and Jared pick up their tickets at the theater on the night of the play, the ticket stubs will become the receipts.

☐ Activities for April 20

24. Two years ago, the Hoffmans had deposited $1,400.00 in a two-year certificate of deposit. Now that the two-year term is up, the CD is worth $1,500 and they must decide what to do with the money. They could **roll over**, or reinvest, the money into a new CD that will pay 2.5% interest. Instead, they decide to invest it in a mutual fund that Jared has researched using the Internet and financial magazines. This particular fund is made up of several steadily growing stocks and has been earning an average interest rate near 8% for the past three years.

    Jared fills out a simple application form, showing how he wants to invest the money. He then sends the application and a check for $1,500.00 to the company that manages the mutual fund, Foster & Stern Investments. Record both a deposit of $1,500.00 (from the CD) and a $1,500.00 check in the *Financial Record Book* or CJH_FINR file and in the checkbook register.

CHECKPOINT

Why did Jared decide to invest the $1,500.00 in the mutual fund rather than roll over the money into another CD?

☐ Activities for April 21

25. Jared is running errands. He stops to pick up some groceries at Family Foods. Record a debit card payment of $67.82 in the *Financial Record Book* or CJH_FINR file and in the checkbook register. File the receipt (Form 85, page 139).
26. Next, Jared stops at Capital and pays $32.72 for gas. Then he picks up the dry cleaning. He pays cash but does not get a receipt. Jared started the day with $100.00 in his wallet. When he gets home he has $20.03. Record cash payments of $32.72 for gasoline and $47.25 for dry cleaning in the *Financial Record Book* or CJH_FINR file. File the receipt (Form 86, page 139).

☐ Activities for April 24

27. Jared and Celina have agreed to meet Rania and Kyle at The Bistro, a casual restaurant near the theater. Jared wants to be sure they have enough cash to pay for dinner, so he stops at the bank on the way to dinner. He uses his debit card to withdraw $200.00 from their checking account. Record the withdrawal in the checkbook register but not in the *Financial Record Book* or CJH_FINR file because he hasn't actually spent the money yet. File the ATM receipt (Form 87, page 141).
28. Celina and Jared enjoy having dinner with Rania and Kyle at The Bistro. Record a cash payment of $47.17 plus a tip of $9.00 in the *Financial Record Book* or CJH_FINR file. Write the amount of the tip on the receipt (Form 88, page 141). Then file the receipt. File the theater ticket stubs (Form 89, page 141) under *Receipts*.

☐ Activities for April 25

29. It is time for Jared's annual eye examination. Because he has vision care insurance, Jared will pay only $30.00 for his eye exam. Record a check

to Dr. Daniel Murad in the *Financial Record Book* or CJH_FINR file and in the checkbook register. File the receipt (Form 90, page 143).

☐ Activities for April 26

30. Jared pays both car loans. Record one check for $216.40 to Lancaster State Bank and one check for $240.60 to Oak Grove Bank in the *Financial Record Book* or CJH_FINR file and in the checkbook register. File the payment slips that would accompany the checks (Form 91, page 143 and Form 92, page 145) under *Checks Written*. Next month, Celina and Jared will arrange new payment plans so that they can pay off their cars more quickly.

☐ Activities for April 27

31. Jared stops at a discount drugstore to pick up some personal care items. Record a check for $57.70 to Chandler in the *Financial Record Book* or CJH_FINR file and in the checkbook register. File the receipt (Form 93, page 145).

☐ Activities for April 28

32. Once every six months, Jared and Celina must pay their property taxes. Because the amount is rather large, they set aside $275.00 each month. Setting money aside enables them to pay the bill when it's due. Record a check for $1,650.00 to Grant County in the *Financial Record Book* or CJH_FINR file and in the checkbook register. File the two portions of the bill (Form 94, page 147) in the appropriate sections of the file folder.

CHECKPOINT

How does payment of property taxes impact the Hoffmans' monthly budget for the *Home* category?

☐ Activities for April 29

33. Celina and Jared have continued to discuss their many investment options. In addition to opening the 401(k) account and putting money in a mutual fund, they've decided to look for a larger house.

Jared goes to their bank to get a home loan qualifying application. This form is not a true loan application, but rather a preliminary form to find out if they will qualify for a home loan. Retrieve Form 95 from page 149 and follow along as Jared fills out the form.

a. Using information from page 37, fill out as much of the top portion as you can. Jared will be the Applicant, and Celina will be the Co-Applicant.
b. Jared's work phone is 419-555-3200 and business address is 225 Chase Street, Maplewood, OH 44922. Celina's business address is their home address. She uses her cell phone as her work phone.
c. Use the information that appears on page 37 to fill in their annual salaries in the Income Information section.
d. Use the checkbook register to fill in the amount currently in their checking account. To fill in their other Assets, use the information given for determining the Hoffmans' net worth. Remember that the $1,500.00 that used to be in a CD is now in a mutual fund.

✔ MATH CHECK

The checkbook register should show $990.88 in their checking account at this point.

e. Under Liabilities, fill in their Mortgage Payment ($830.00). Although they pay off their credit card bill each month, Jared estimates that they charge an average of $100 on the card each month. Record $100 for Credit Card Debt. For Other Loans, fill in the total of their two monthly car payments shown in their budget ($457.00).
f. Sign and date the form as if you were both Jared and Celina. Jared will return this form to the bank, but you should file it under Forms.

☐ Activities for April 30

34. Record the direct deposit of Jared's paycheck for $1,515.76 in the *Financial Record Book* or

Illustration 23: Jared's Paycheck Receipt Showing his 401(k) Contribution

Maplewood Medical Center

225 Chase Street
Maplewood, OH 44922
(419) 555-3200

Direct Payroll Deposit

Employee:

Jared Hoffman
363 Sherwood Circle
Maplewood, OH 44922
(419) 555-4576
SSN: ###-##-0018

Payroll Period:	4/16/20-- to 4/30/20--
Check Date:	4/30/20--
Gross Pay:	$2,250.00
Deductions:	
Federal	$216.35
Social Security	139.50
Medicare	32.63
State	71.26
Health Insurance	142.00
Dental	12.00
Vision	8.00
401(k) 5%	112.50
Net Pay:	$1,515.76
Deposited to:	334-067214

CJH_FINR file and in the checkbook register. Notice that Jared's net pay is less than it was the last time because of his 401(k) contribution (Illustration 23). Also record a deposit of $3,700.00 for Celina's earnings for the month.

FYI *Notice that only the last four digits of Jared's Social Security number appear on Jared's paycheck receipt in Illustration 23. This is often done to help protect the employee's identity.*

35. Using Form 96 (pages 151–152), reconcile the Hoffmans' checking account. Because this statement was prepared on April 28, there will be four outstanding checks and two outstanding deposits not shown on this statement. This account was charged a fee of $7.00 and does not earn any interest. Refer to the directions for reconciling Adam's checking account on page 33 if you need help. After reconciling the account, be sure to record the service charge in the *Financial Record Book* or CJH_FINR file and in the checkbook register.

36. To prove cash in the *Financial Record Book,* you first must reconstruct the Hoffmans' cash transactions.

✔ MATH CHECK

You should have arrived at $193.47 cash remaining.

Using this information and your final checking account balance, prove cash in the *Financial Record Book* or CJH_FINR file.

Refer to the directions for proving Adam's cash on page 37 if you need help. Be sure to enter the column totals at the bottom of the second page of the *Financial Record Book.*

✔ Math Check

Remember that the two ending balances will be $116.34 apart because the two credit card transactions have not yet been paid by check.

CHECKPOINT

Why is it important to record credit card transactions in the Financial Record when they occur rather than when they are paid?

Jump$tart Coalition for Personal Financial Literacy

National Standards in K-12 Personal Finance Education

Planning and Money Management

Standard 7: *Examine the purpose and importance of a will.*

A will describes how you want your property distributed when you die. If you die without a will, state law dictates what happens to your belongings.

Parents can use a will to name a guardian for their children. Although courts are not bound by this part of a will, it is a good way to let the court know about your wishes.

Activities

1. Each state determines who may make a valid will. Research the requirements for your state or a neighboring state.
2. Based on the law in your state, briefly explain what happens to a person's property when there is no valid will.

Special Topics

Locate the following Special Topic readings on the Data CD. Read the article and answer the Think It Through questions that appear at the end of the article.

- Special Topic 10: How Your Money Can Earn More Money
- Special Topic 11: Introduction to Investing
- Special Topic 12: Why You Need a Will

Forms

Forms for Part 2

Forms for Part 3

Forms for Part 4

Form 1

STATEMENT OF NET WORTH FOR ____________________

Assets		Liabilities and Net Worth	
Checking Account		Car Loan	
Savings Account		Rent Due	
Savings Bond		Gas/Electric Bill	
Car		Phone Bill	
Personal Items		Total Liabilities	
Cash		Net Worth	
Total Assets		Total Liabilities and Net Worth	

Form 2

BUDGET WORKSHEET FOR ____________________

Monthly Income

Gross Pay .... ________
Taxes/Deductions .... ________
Net Pay .... ________

Monthly Expenses

Savings/Debt Payoff .... ________
Savings Accounts .... ________
Investments .... ________
Loan Payments .... ________
Other (________________) ________

Home .... ________
Rent/Mortgage Payment ..... ________
Property Taxes .... ________
Utilities .... ________
Phone/Pager Services .... ________
Cable/Satellite TV Service .... ________
Internet Service .... ________
Home Maintenance .... ________
Home/Renter's Insurance ..... ________
Home Furnishings............... ________
Home Electronics .... ________

Food/Sundries .... ________
Food .... ________
Personal Care Items .... ________
Small Home Care Items .... ________

Personal .... ________
Clothes & Shoes .... ________
Haircuts/Salon Services .... ________
Dry Cleaning/Laundry.......... ________
Gym Membership............... ________
Life Insurance .... ________

Column 1 Total .... ________

Transportation .... ________
Car Loan Payment .... ________
Car Insurance .... ________
Gasoline/Oil .... ________
Car Maintenance .... ________
License/Registration Fees ..... ________
Bus/Subway Fares .... ________

Entertainment .... ________
Restaurant Meals .... ________
Event Fees/Tickets .... ________
Travel Expenses .... ________

Miscellaneous .... ________
Child Care Expenses .... ________
Gifts .... ________
Donations/Charities .... ________
Pet/Hobby Expenses .... ________
Education Fees .... ________
Bank Service Charges........... ________

Health Care .... ________
Doctor & Dental Fees .... ________
Prescription Medicines......... ________
Glasses/Contact Lenses .... ________

Column 2 Total .... ________
Grand Total .... ________

Form 3

Water Point Grille

Earnings Statement

5101 Lakeland Blvd.
Maplewood, OH 44921

Check Issued: 10/1/--
Pay Period: 9/1/-- to 9/30/--
Tyra M. Burns
4500 Red Maple Lane, Apt. 115
Maplewood, OH 44920
SSN: 333-22-8888

	This Period	Year-to-Date
Gross Pay	$2,700.00	$21,600.00
Deductions		
Federal Income Tax	296.25	2,370.00
Social Security Tax	167.40	1,339.20
State Income Tax	75.00	600.00
City Income Tax	70.20	561.60
Medicare Tax	39.15	313.20
Health Insurance	135.00	1,080.00
Net Pay	$1,917.00	$15,336.00

Water Point Grille

1283

5101 Lakeland Blvd.
Maplewood, OH 44921

DATE 10/1/-- 12-34/567

PAY TO THE ORDER OF TYRA M. BURNS $ 1,917.00

ONE THOUSAND NINE HUNDRED SEVENTEEN AND 00/100 ------------ DOLLARS

LKB Bank

Thomas Connelly

⑆999955555⑆⑆000⑈000⑈

Form 4

Tyra M. Burns
4500 Red Maple Lane, Apt. 115
Maplewood, OH 44920

Acct. No.	248–2A
Amount Due	$42.53
Date Due	10/10/--

TCG&E

Tri-County Gas & Electric
P.O. Box 13579
Maplewood, OH 44920

Detach and return this portion with your payment.

BILLING EXPLANATION

BILLING PERIOD	ITEM	CURRENT CHARGES
9/1 – 9/30	Gas Meter #3077	$11.30
	Electricity Meter #62809B	31.23

Questions? Please call 419-555-4679 for service.

TRI-COUNTY GAS & ELECTRIC

Form 3

ENDORSE HERE

Form 5

Tyra M. Burns
4500 Red Maple Lane, Apt. 115
Maplewood, OH 44920

Maplewood Telephone Co.

Account No. 1–419–555–2010

Amount Due by 10/12/-- $35.95

Maplewood Telephone Co.
Dept. 1919
Maplewood, OH 44930-1919

Save this portion for your records.

Last Month	
Previous Bill Amount	$34.22
Payment Received	$34.22
Last Month's Balance	$ 0.00

This Month	
Monthly Service	$21.06
Monthly Maintenance	$ 2.00
Federal Tax	$ 1.86
Long Distance Service	$11.03
Total Due	$35.95

Thank You for Choosing

Maplewood Telephone Co.

Form 6

```
*** U.S. POSTAL SERVICE ***
MAPLEWOOD              14916
067890                 33.00
ARLIS                   # 05
10-06               12:06:21
----------------------------
      CUSTOMER RECEIPT
----------------------------
090 POSTAGE STAMPS    11.40
                   ---------
  TOTAL                11.40
  CASH T               20.00
                   ---------
  CHANGE                8.60
----------------------------
     *** THANK YOU ***
----------------------------
```

Form 7

Park
Department Stores

Today's Date	10/8
JACKET Item #66270	$99.00
SKIRT Item #23142	$56.00
SKIRT	$42.00
SUBTOTAL	$141.00
6% TAX	$8.46
TOTAL	$149.46
CHECK #104	$149.46

Refunds & Exchanges Require Receipt

Form 8

THANK YOU FOR SHOPPING
LI'S MARKET

LETTUCE	0.68 LB @ 1.64/LB	1.12
KIWI	4/1.50	1.50
MUSHROOMS	0.32 LB @ 2.73/LB	.87
CANTALOUPE	1 @ 1.99	1.99
BANANAS	0.79 LB @ .54/LB	.43
GRAPES	1.66 LB @ 2.19/LB	3.64
ORANGES	3/1.25	1.25

TOTAL	$40.80
CASH GIVEN	$50.00
CHANGE DUE	$9.20

Form 9

FCB **First City Bank**

Debit Card Application

NAME ______________________________

ADDRESS ______________________________

____

PHONE # ________________ **SOC. SEC. #** ________________

EMPLOYER ______________________________

EMPLOYER PHONE # ________________

OCCUPATION ______________________________

YEARS EMPLOYED ____________

CHECKING ACCOUNT NO. ______________________________

MOTHER'S MAIDEN NAME ______________________________

SIGNATURE ________________________ **DATE** ____________

This form authorizes First City Bank to issue a debit card in connection with the checking account listed above. A personal identification number (PIN) will be assigned to you.

Form 10

FCB First City Bank

Withdrawal Receipt

DATE:	10/9/--
ACCOUNT NO.:	12-345678
AMOUNT WITHDRAWN:	$150.00
ACCOUNT BALANCE:	$1,829.18

Form 11

East Bay Community College

Date: *October 11, --*
Game Time: *7:30 p.m.*
Cost: *$10.00*
Seat: *Sect B–12A*

East Bay Buccaneers vs. Kirkwood Knights

Form 12

John Rasgotra, M.D.
321 State Blvd., Suite 6B
Maplewood, OH 44920

Receipt No. 50831

Received from: Tyra M. Burns

Amount: $25

Method of Payment: check

Date: 10/12/--

Received by: Anna Marie Palmisano

Form 13

RECEIPT

DATE: 10/15/--

PAID TO: Lydia D. Burns

PAID BY: Tyra M. Burns

FOR: Car loan payment

AMOUNT: $200

SIGNED: Lydia D. Burns

Form 14

DATE	TIME	MACHINE
1017	9:32AM	BX805

DEPOSIT TO CHECKING $85.00

BALANCE $1,889.18

FCB First City Bank

Form 15

Levi's Gas

1600 Chippewa Ave
Maplewood OH 44920

10/18/-- 05:48 PM PUMP 07

GASOLINE $34.83

TOTAL $34.83

CASH GIVEN $40.00

CHANGE $ 5.17

THANK YOU!
PLEASE COME AGAIN

Form 16

MANUFACTURER'S COUPON | EXPIRES 12/31

25¢ OFF

On your next purchase of any size Twin Circle Cream Cheese

Form 16

MANUFACTURER'S COUPON | NO EXPIRATION DATE

SAVE $1.00 ON 2

Osage Frozen Pizzas

Coupon Savings

Form 16

MANUFACTURER'S COUPON | EXPIRES 2/14

SAVE 75¢

when you buy 3 cartons of

Happy & Healthy Yogurt

Form 17

WELCOME TO
HOLLAND'S GROCERIES

REGISTER: 6 DATE: 10/19

MILK	1.99
YOGURT X 3	2.57
BAKERY	2.99
FRZN O.J.	1.29
FRZN PIZZA	5.99
TOILET PAPER*	3.75
FRZN PIZZA	5.99
CRM CHEESE	2.29
TOOTHPASTE*	2.18
SUBTOTAL	54.92
*6% TAX	.36
COUPON	.75-
COUPON	1.00-
COUPON	.25-
TOTAL	53.28
DEBIT CARD	53.28
CHANGE	.00

Form 18

Zhang's Garage

13413 Tanglewood Dr.
Maplewood, OH 44923
(419) 555-1341

Customer Information

TYRA M. BURNS
4500 RED MAPLE LANE, APT. 115
MAPLEWOOD, OH 44920
(419) 555-2010

Car: 04 ASTER COUPE | *Mileage:* 67,496

Item	*Description*	*Parts*	*Labor*	*Charge*
1	OIL CHANGE	7.04	25.00	32.04

Subtotal	32.04
Tax	1.92
Total	33.96
Paid	33.96

Tyra M. Burns
Customer Signature

Form 19

Tally Toys

PUZZLE Item #61616	$18.39
Subtotal	$18.39
Tax	$ 1.10
Amount Due	$19.49
Check	$19.49
Change Due	$ 0.00

Form 20

Customer Information:

Tyra M. Burns
4500 Red Maple Lane, Apt. 115
Maplewood, OH 44920

Account Information:

Account Number: RTD212
Date Due: 10/30/--
Amount Due: $120.00

Remit To:

Latero Insurance
P.O. Box 6238
Indianapolis, IN 46206-6238

Keep this portion for your records.

Latero Insurance

Tyra M. Burns
4500 Red Maple Lane, Apt. 115
Maplewood, OH 44920

Account Number: RTD212
Date Due: 10/30/--

Description	Amount
Automobile Insurance	$120.00
Total:	$120.00

Form 21

Harper's Salon

Haircut.................... $25.00
Color....................... $38.00

Amount Due $63.00
Cash Given.......... $63.00
Change Due .... $ 0.00

Thank You

Form 22

DATE	TIME	MACHINE
1028	1:17PM	BX805

WITHDRAW FROM CHECKING $150.00
BALANCE $1,312.45

FCB First City Bank

Form 23

Tabla de Cena
Mexican Restaurant

DATE: 10/28 SERVER: ROB

SALAD	$ 3.75
FAJITA DINNER	$15.95
SOFT DRINK	$ 3.50
SOPAPILLAS	$ 4.50
SUBTOTAL	$27.70
TAX	1.66
TOTAL DUE	$29.36

Form 23

GRAND BALLET TOUR

Souvenir Program (including tax)....$5.00

Total...............................$5.00

Cash Tendered.......................$5.00

Change..............................$0.00

Form 23

Grand Ballet Tour

VENUE: Maplewood Civic Center

DATE: October 28, 20--

TIME: Evening, 8:00 PM

SEAT LOCATION

ROW: C SEAT: 201

EVENT CODE: DQH9B38F

ADDMISSION: $70.00

(Admission price includes all taxes and fees.)

Form 24

FCB First City Bank

Savings Deposit

Date ____________

Deposited to the Account of:

____________________ Amount $ ________

______________________________ Dollars

Acct. No. [ ][ ]-[ ][ ][ ][ ][ ][ ]

____
Signature

FCB First City Bank

TYRA M. BURNS
4500 RED MAPLE LANE. APT. 115
MAPLEWOOD, OH 44920

Statement For:	9/29/-- to 10/29/--
Beginning Balance:	$740.12
Ending Balance:	$1,082.45
Account Number:	12-345678

Checks

Check No.	Date Paid	Amount
101	10/5	450.00
102	10/8	42.53
103	10/8	35.95
104	10/11	149.46
105	10/14	25.00

Check No.	Date Paid	Amount
106	10/18	200.00
108	10/23	33.96
109	10/25	19.49
110	10/26	120.00
111	10/29	220.00

Debits and Withdrawals

Date	Amount	Description
10/9	150.00	Withdrawal
10/19	53.28	Debit card payment Holland's Groceries
10/28	150.00	ATM cash withdrawal
10/29	10.00	Service charge

Deposits

Date	Amount	Description
10/2	1,917.00	Deposit
10/17	85.00	ATM Deposit

Form 26

STATEMENT OF NET WORTH FOR ____________________

Assets		Liabilities and Net Worth	
Checking Account		Rent Due	
Savings Account		Gas/Electric Bill	
401(k) Account		Phone Bill	
Life Insurance Policy		Cable TV & Internet	
Car		Insurance Bill	
Personal Items		Total Liabilities	
Cash		Net Worth	
Total Assets		Total Liabilities and Net Worth	

Form 27

BUDGET WORKSHEET FOR ____________________

Monthly Income

Gross Pay .... ________
Taxes/Deductions .... ________
Net Pay .... ________

Monthly Expenses

Savings/Debt Payoff .... ________
Savings Accounts .... ________
Investments .... ________
Loan Payments .... ________
Other (________________) ________

Home .... ________
Rent/Mortgage Payment ..... ________
Property Taxes .... ________
Utilities .... ________
Phone/Pager Services .... ________
Cable/Satellite TV Service .... ________
Internet Service .... ________
Home Maintenance .... ________
Home/Renter's Insurance .... ________
Home Furnishings .... ________
Home Electronics .... ________

Food/Sundries .... ________
Food .... ________
Personal Care Items .... ________
Small Home Care Items .... ________

Personal .... ________
Clothes & Shoes .... ________
Haircuts/Salon Services .... ________
Dry Cleaning/Laundry .... ________
Gym Membership .... ________
Life Insurance .... ________

Transportation .... ________
Car Loan Payment .... ________
Car Insurance .... ________
Gasoline/Oil .... ________
Car Maintenance .... ________
License/Registration Fees ..... ________
Bus/Subway Fares .... ________

Entertainment .... ________
Restaurant Meals .... ________
Event Fees/Tickets .... ________
Travel Expenses .... ________

Miscellaneous .... ________
Child Care Expenses .... ________
Gifts .... ________
Donations/Charities .... ________
Pet/Hobby Expenses .... ________
Education Fees .... ________
Bank Service Charge .... ________

Health Care .... ________
Doctor & Dental Fees .... ________
Prescription Medicines .... ________
Glasses/Contact Lenses .... ________

Column 1 Total .... ________

Column 2 Total .... ________
Grand Total .... ________

Cabot Services, Inc.

8820 Main Street
Hopewell, OH 45311
(937) 555-3777

Adam G. Warner
4412 Lincoln Ave
Hopewell, OH 45313
SSN: 111-55-9999

Direct Deposit Paycheck Receipt
(This is not a check.)

Date Issued: 3/1/--
Amount Deposited: $1,737.51

Pay	This Period	YTD
Gross Pay	$2,500.00	$10,000.00
Net Pay	$1,737.51	$ 6,950.04

Deductions	This Period	YTD
401(k)	$150.00	$600.00
Federal Tax	$231.21	$924.84
State Tax	$ 79.98	$319.92
Soc. Sec.	$155.00	$620.00
Medicare	$ 36.25	$145.00
PPO Health Plan	$110.05	$440.20

Deposited to:
Hopewell Community Bank
Checking account #: 21-436587

Form 29

Easy-Fix Car Care

DATE: 3/3 TIME: 12:15

OIL CHANGE	32.99
AIR FILTER	18.69
SUBTOTAL	51.68
TAX	3.10
TOTAL	54.78

Form 30

Adam G. Warner
4412 Lincoln Ave
Hopewell, OH 45313

Acct. No.	227–7A
Amount Due	$105.10
Date Due	3/7/--

HEI

Hopewell Energy, Inc.
P.O. Box 13579
Hopewell OH 45301

Detach and return this portion with your payment.

BILLING EXPLANATION

BILLING PERIOD	ITEM	CURRENT CHARGES
2/1 – 2/28	Gas Meter #6389	$38.12
	Electricity Meter #83114A	$66.98

Questions? Please call 937-555-4679 for service.

HOPEWELL ENERGY, INC.

Form 31

PBC Telephone Co.

Adam G. Warner
4412 Lincoln Ave
Hopewell, OH 45313

Account No. 1–937–555–2262

Amount Due by 3/8/-- $34.31

PBC Telephone Co.
Dept. 2581
Hopewell, OH 45313

File this portion with your records.

Last Month	
Previous Bill Amount	$32.85
Payment Received	$32.85
Last Month's Balance	$ 0.00
This Month	
Monthly Service	$22.59
Monthly Maintenance	$ 1.15
Federal Tax	$ .68
Long Distance Service	$ 9.89
Total Due	***$34.31***

PBC Telephone Co.

You can rely on us!

Form 32

Express Cable Service

Customer:

Adam G. Warner
4412 Lincoln Ave
Hopewell, OH 45313

Express Cable Service
23 S. Third Street
Hopewell, OH 45313

Keep this statement for your records.

Sports and Movie Premium Package	$84.75
E-Express Internet Service	$44.45
Tax	$ 7.75

Amount Due: $136.95

Date Due: 3/12/--

Express Cable Service

Stay tuned for special offers on premium channels next month!

Form 33

GasCo

Date: 3/6
Station: 618
Pump: 2

Regular Gas	$35.24

Charged to WorldCard **** 9867

Save this receipt for your records.

Form 34

THANK YOU FOR SHOPPING
HILLTOP GROCERY STORE

STACI WAS YOUR CASHIER.
DATE 3/6 TIME 5:52

CEREAL	4.25
PARMESAN CHEESE	4.12
BREAD	2.79
DELI	3.29
MILK	2.99
GR TURKEY	2.31
1.01 LB @ 2.29/LB	
SUBTOTAL	$78.15
*TAX	$1.18
TOTAL	$79.33
DEBIT	$79.33

Form 35

JASON'S GARAGE

15692 FIFTH ST., HOPEWELL, OH 45313
(937) 555-8020

CUSTOMER NAME: ADAM WARNER		PHONE: 555-2262
CAR MAKE: MERIDIAN	MODEL: SE	YEAR: 2000

ESTIMATE	LABOR - 3 HRS@$50/HR	$150.00
	PARTS	$ 35.00
	CUSTOMER'S INITIAL: AGW	$ 185.00
SERVICE		

TOTAL DUE	
TOTAL PAID	

Form **1040A** Department of the Treasury—Internal Revenue Service
U.S. Individual Income Tax Return 20--
IRS Use Only—Do not write or staple in this space.

OMB No. 1545-0074

Label
(See page 15.)

Use the IRS label. Otherwise, please print or type.

LABEL HERE

Your first name and initial	Last name	Your social security number
If a joint return, spouse's first name and initial	Last name	Spouse's social security number
Home address (number and street). If you have a P.O. box, see page 15.	Apt. no.	▲ You **must** enter your SSN(s) above. ▲
City, town or post office, state, and ZIP code. If you have a foreign address, see page 15.		Checking a box below will not change your tax or refund.

Presidential Election Campaign ▶ Check here if you, or your spouse if filing jointly, want $3 to go to this fund (see page 15) ▶ ☐ **You** ☐ **Spouse**

Filing status
Check only one box.

1 ☐ Single
2 ☐ Married filing jointly (even if only one had income)
3 ☐ Married filing separately. Enter spouse's SSN above and full name here. ▶
4 ☐ Head of household (with qualifying person). (See page 16.) If the qualifying person is a child but not your dependent, enter this child's name here. ▶
5 ☐ Qualifying widow(er) with dependent child (see page 17)

Exemptions
6a ☐ **Yourself.** If someone can claim you as a dependent, **do not** check box 6a.
b ☐ **Spouse**

Boxes checked on 6a and 6b ____

c **Dependents:**

If more than six dependents, see page 18.

(1) First name Last name	(2) Dependent's social security number	(3) Dependent's relationship to you	(4) ✓ if qualifying child for child tax credit (see page 18)
			☐
			☐
			☐
			☐
			☐
			☐

No. of children on 6c who:
- **lived with you** ____
- **did not live with you due to divorce or separation (see page 19)** ____

Dependents on 6c not entered above ____

d Total number of exemptions claimed. **Add numbers on lines above** ▶ ☐

Income
Attach Form(s) W-2 here. Also attach Form(s) 1099-R if tax was withheld.

If you did not get a W-2, see page 21.

Enclose, but do not attach, any payment.

7	Wages, salaries, tips, etc. Attach Form(s) W-2.		7
8a	**Taxable** interest. Attach Schedule 1 if required.		8a
b	**Tax-exempt** interest. **Do not** include on line 8a.	8b	
9a	Ordinary dividends. Attach Schedule 1 if required.		9a
b	Qualified dividends (see page 22).	9b	
10	Capital gain distributions (see page 22).		10
11a	IRA distributions. 11a	11b Taxable amount (see page 22).	11b
12a	Pensions and annuities. 12a	12b Taxable amount (see page 23).	12b
13	Unemployment compensation and Alaska Permanent Fund dividends.		13
14a	Social security benefits. 14a	14b Taxable amount (see page 25).	14b
15	Add lines 7 through 14b (far right column). This is your **total income.** ▶		15

Adjusted gross income

16	Educator expenses (see page 25).	16	
17	IRA deduction (see page 27).	17	
18	Student loan interest deduction (see page 29).	18	
19	Tuition and fees deduction. Attach Form 8917.	19	
20	Add lines 16 through 19. These are your **total adjustments.**		20
21	Subtract line 20 from line 15. This is your **adjusted gross income.** ▶		21

For Disclosure, Privacy Act, and Paperwork Reduction Act Notice, see page 74. Cat. No. 11327A Form **1040A** (20--)

Form 1040A (20_ _) Page **2**

Tax, credits, and payments

22 Enter the amount from line 21 (adjusted gross income). 22

23a Check if: { ☐ **You** were born before January 2, 1943, ☐ Blind } **Total boxes checked** ▶ 23a ☐
☐ **Spouse** was born before January 2, 1943, ☐ Blind

b If you are married filing separately and your spouse itemizes deductions, see page 30 and check here ▶ 23b ☐

Standard Deduction for—

- People who checked any box on line 23a or 23b **or** who can be claimed as a dependent, see page 30.
- All others:

Single or Married filing separately, $5,350

Married filing jointly or Qualifying widow(er), $10,700

Head of household, $7,850

24 Enter your **standard deduction** (see left margin). 24

25 Subtract line 24 from line 22. If line 24 is more than line 22, enter -0-. 25

26 If line 22 is $117,300 or less, multiply $3,400 by the total number of exemptions claimed on line 6d. If line 22 is over $117,300, see the worksheet on page 32. 26

27 Subtract line 26 from line 25. If line 26 is more than line 25, enter -0-. This is your **taxable income.** ▶ 27

28 **Tax,** including any alternative minimum tax (see page 30). 28

29 Credit for child and dependent care expenses. Attach Schedule 2. 29

30 Credit for the elderly or the disabled. Attach Schedule 3. 30

31 Education credits. Attach Form 8863. 31

32 Child tax credit (see page 35). Attach Form 8901 if required. 32

33 Retirement savings contributions credit. Attach Form 8880. 33

34 Add lines 29 through 33. These are your **total credits.** 34

35 Subtract line 34 from line 28. If line 34 is more than line 28, enter -0-. 35

36 Advance earned income credit payments from Form(s) W-2, box 9. 36

37 Add lines 35 and 36. This is your **total tax.** ▶ 37

38 Federal income tax withheld from Forms W-2 and 1099. 38

39 20_ _ estimated tax payments and amount applied from 20_ _ return. 39

If you have a qualifying child, attach Schedule EIC.

40a **Earned income credit (EIC).** 40a

b Nontaxable combat pay election. 40b

41 Additional child tax credit. Attach Form 8812. 41

42 Add lines 38, 39, 40a, and 41. These are your **total payments.** ▶ 42

Refund

43 If line 42 is more than line 37, subtract line 37 from line 42. This is the amount you **overpaid.** 43

Direct deposit? See page 52 and fill in 44b, 44c, and 44d or Form 8888.

44a Amount of line 43 you want **refunded to you.** If Form 8888 is attached, check here ▶ ☐ 44a

▶ b Routing number ☐☐☐☐☐☐☐☐☐ ▶ **c** Type: ☐ Checking ☐ Savings

▶ d Account number ☐☐☐☐☐☐☐☐☐☐☐☐☐☐☐☐☐

45 Amount of line 43 you want **applied to your 20_ _ estimated tax.** 45

Amount you owe

46 **Amount you owe.** Subtract line 42 from line 37. For details on how to pay, see page 53. ▶ 46

47 Estimated tax penalty (see page 53). 47

Third party designee

Do you want to allow another person to discuss this return with the IRS (see page 54)? ☐ **Yes.** Complete the following. ☐ **No**

Designee's name ▶ Phone no. ▶ ( ) Personal identification number (PIN) ▶ ☐☐☐☐☐

Sign here

Joint return? See page 15.

Keep a copy for your records.

Under penalties of perjury, I declare that I have examined this return and accompanying schedules and statements, and to the best of my knowledge and belief, they are true, correct, and accurately list all amounts and sources of income I received during the tax year. Declaration of preparer (other than the taxpayer) is based on all information of which the preparer has any knowledge.

Your signature	Date	Your occupation	Daytime phone number ( )
Spouse's signature. If a joint return, **both** must sign.	Date	Spouse's occupation	

Paid preparer's use only

Preparer's signature ▶	Date	Check if self-employed ☐	Preparer's SSN or PTIN
Firm's name (or yours if self-employed), address, and ZIP code ▶		EIN	
		Phone no. ( )	

Form **1040A** (20_ _)

JASON'S GARAGE

15692 FIFTH ST., HOPEWELL, OH 45313
(937) 555-8020

CUSTOMER NAME: ADAM WARNER		PHONE: 555-2262
CAR MAKE: MERIDIAN	MODEL: SE	YEAR: 2000

ESTIMATE		
	LABOR - 3 HRS @ $50/HR	$150.00
	PARTS	$ 35.00
	CUSTOMER'S INITIAL: AGW	$185.00

SERVICE		
	LABOR - 3 HRS @ $50/HR	$150.00
	ACTUAL PARTS	$ 40.00
	SUBTOTAL	$190.00
	TAX	$ 11.40

TOTAL DUE	$201.40
TOTAL PAID	$201.40

Hopewell Community Bank

Credit/Loan Application

Form 38

Branch ______________________

Purpose (This application may NOT be used for either a line of credit secured by residential real estate or a variable rate installment loan secured by principal residence.)

Amount Requested	Terms Requested

Applicant Information

Last Name	First Name	Mid. Initi. Suffix
(Business Loan Only) Business Name		
Address		
Address		
City	State/ ZIP Code	
County	Length of Residence Years Months	
Phone	Social Security No.	
Birth Date	No. of Dependents	
Previous Residence *(If less than 2 years)*		
City	State/ ZIP Code	
Length of Residence Years Months		

Employer	
Occupation	
Phone	Length Employed Years Months
Previous Employer *(If less than 2 years)*	
Occupation	
Phone	Length Employed Years Months
Gross Salary	Weekly (W) Biweekly (B) Monthly (M) Annually (A) (circle one)
Other Income (circle one) W B M A	Source
Name of Nearest Relative Not Living With You	
Address	
Phone	Relationship

Checking/Savings Accounts

Bank Name	Account Number	Account Type
Bank Name	Account Number	Account Type

Credit Experience/Obligations

(i.e., include all existing payments such as credit cards, department stores, bank or finance co. loans, and other obligations such as alimony, child support or separate maintenance, guarantees or co-maker on loans.)

Creditor	Account Number	Balance	Monthly Payment	To Be Paid Off With This Loan (Yes/No)
( ) Mortgage ( ) Rent ( ) Other				
Second Mortgage/ Home Equity				
If Real Estate Owned: Date of Purchase	Purchase Price	Current Market Value		
Auto Year of Auto Make of Auto				
Auto Year of Auto Make of Auto				

If I do not qualify for credit with you, I authorize you to consider my application under the terms and conditions of any applicable alternative loan program. Such loan may be sold to another lender with which you have a relationship. I authorize you to forward my application and other documentation to that lender and understand that the terms and conditions may differ from those for which I am currently applying.

☐ I am not interested in having my application considered for an alternative loan program.

Applicant's Signature	Date

Form 39

Talia's
Pizza & Pasta

Date: 3/11
Time: 6:57

Dinner	$14.99
Child's Dinner	$ 7.99
Drink	$ 2.50
Child's Drink	$ 1.50
Subtotal	$26.98
Tax	$ 1.62
Total	$28.60
Amount Given	$30.00
Change Due	$ 1.40

Form 40

GasCo

Date: 3/6
Station: 618
Pump: 8

Regular Gas	**$34.41**

Charged to WorldCard ** 9867**

Save this receipt for your records.

Form 41

Fiori's Drug Store

DINO BANDAGES	4.39
LOTION	5.65
DEODORANT	1.97
FACIAL TISSUE	2.89
GREETING CARD	3.10
GREETING CARD	.99
MAGAZINE	4.50
SUBTOTAL	23.49
TAX	1.41
TOTAL DUE	24.90
AMOUNT GIVEN	40.00
CHANGE DUE	15.10

Thank You

Form 42

THANK YOU FOR SHOPPING
HILLTOP GROCERY STORE

DARRELL WAS YOUR CASHIER.
DATE 3/14 TIME 7:36

SPAGHETTI	1.29
GREEN BEANS	1.42
0.89 LB @ 1.59/LB	
BANANAS	.72
1.05 LB @ .69/LB	
COFFEE	5.99
TUNA	5.48
2 @ 2.74	

SUBTOTAL	$69.51
*TAX	$.98
TOTAL	$70.49
DEBIT	$70.49

Form 43

CHILDREN'S MUSEUM AND ACTIVITY CENTER

ADMIT 1 ADULT

DATE: 3/15 **PRICE: $10.00**

CHILDREN'S MUSEUM AND ACTIVITY CENTER

ADMIT 1 CHILD

DATE: 3/15 **PRICE: $8.00**

Form 44

Welcome to
CHILDREN'S MUSEUM AND ACTIVITY CENTER Restaurant

SANDWICH	$4.50
HOT DOG	$3.25
FRUIT	$1.49
DRINK	$1.15
CHIPS	$1.15
DRINK	$1.15
SUBTOTAL	$12.69
TAX	$ .76
TOTAL	$13.45
AMOUNT PAID	$13.45

THANK YOU! COME AGAIN!

Form 45

Cabot Services, Inc.

8820 Main Street
Hopewell, OH 45311
(937) 555-3777

Adam G. Warner
4412 Lincoln Ave
Hopewell, OH 45313
SSN: 111-55-9999

Direct Deposit Paycheck Receipt
(This is not a check.)

Date Issued: 3/15/--

Amount Deposited: $1,737.51

Pay	This Period	YTD
Gross Pay	$2,500.00	$12,500.00
Net Pay	$1,737.51	$ 8,687.55

Deductions	This Period	YTD
401(k)	$150.00	$ 750.00
Federal Tax	$231.21	$1,156.05
State Tax	$ 79.98	$ 399.90
Soc. Sec.	$155.00	$ 775.00
Medicare	$ 36.25	$ 181.25
PPO Health Plan	$110.05	$ 550.25

Deposited to:
Hopewell Community Bank
Checking account #: 21-436587

Form 46

Receipt

Date: 3/17/--

Issued By: Stay & Play Child Care Center

For: Child Care for April

Amount: $620 (Check No. 675)

From: Adam G. Warner (Carson Warner)

Signed: Nicole Quinn

Form 47

Tori Davis-Martinez

From: auto-confirm@stacksetc.com
Sent: March 18, 20—
To: agwarner@expresslink.com
Subject: Your Order with Stacks Etc.

Stacks Etc

VIEW CART | YOUR ACCOUNT | HELP

Thanks for your order, Tori!

Purchase Information:

E-mail Address: agwarner@expresslink.com

Billing Address:
Adam G. Warner
4412 Lincoln Ave
Hopewell, OH 45313
United States
(937) 555-2262

Shipping Address:
Adam G. Warner
4412 Lincoln Ave
Hopewell, OH 45313
United States
(937) 555-2262

Purchase Total **$29.95**

Order Summary:

Shipping Details
Order #: 076-23801
Shipping Method: Standard
Subtotal of Items: $25.00
Shipping & Handling: $ 4.95
Total for This Order: $29.95

Shipping estimate: March 19, 20—
Delivery estimate: March 26, 20—

1 **"Getting Started with BudgetXT"**
Luis Fuentes; paperback; $25.00

Form 48

Adam G. Warner
4412 Lincoln Ave
Hopewell, OH 45313

Due: 3/22/--

Amount: $73.00

S&T Insurance Company
PO Box 276
Columbus, OH 43218

Policy Number	Coverage	Monthly Premium
AGW 373 AUTO	Car Insurance	$45.00
AGW 477 RENT	Renter's Insurance	$16.00
AGW 880 LIFE	Whole Life Insurance	$12.00

Return this portion with your payment.

AGW 373 AUTO	$45.00
AGW 477 RENT	$16.00
AGW 880 LIFE	$12.00
TOTAL	**$73.00**

Due: 3/22/--

S&T Insurance Company
PO Box 276
Columbus, OH 43218

Adam G. Warner
4412 Lincoln Ave
Hopewell, OH 45313

Form 49

Michelle Washio, M.D.
Pediatrician
231 Shane Drive, Suite 4
Hopewell, OH 45311
(937) 555-2727

Date: 3/19 Time: 3:25

Patient's Name: CARSON WARNER

Patient Number: COB - 238

Patient's Address: 4412 LINCOLN AVE, HOPEWELL

Diagnosis: STREP THROAT

Copayment: $25.00

Paid: $25.00 BY CHECK (ADAM G. WARNER)

Signed: *Susan Franks*

Form 50

Fiori's Drug Store

PRESCRIPTION	20.00
PPO PLAN	
SUBTOTAL	20.00
TAX	00.00
TOTAL DUE	20.00
CHECK GIVEN	20.00

Thank You

Form 51

GasCo

Date: 3/21
Station: 618
Pump: 5

Regular Gas	**$33.85**

Charged to WorldCard ** 9867**

Save this receipt for your records.

Form 52

THANK YOU FOR SHOPPING
HILLTOP GROCERY STORE

TAMEKA WAS YOUR CASHIER.
DATE 3/22 TIME 1:15

LUNCH BAGS*	.78
PAPER TOWELS*	1.19
BREAD	2.79
FRZN JUICE	1.09
SOUR CREAM	1.88
DELI	3.85
TOILET PAPER*	3.77
STRAWBERRIES 1 PINT	1.95
SUBTOTAL	$91.42
*TAX	$ 1.72
TOTAL	$92.14
DEBIT	$92.14

Form 53

Delker Clothing

BLAZER #3131 4680 921	$210.00
SUBTOTAL	$210.00
TAX	$12.60
TOTAL	$222.60
CHECK GIVEN	$222.60

Receipt required for refund or exchange.

Form 54

Shamrock Shoes
Where Kids Come First

Date: 3/23
Time: 2:06

Shoes	$16.99
Sandals	$9.85
Subtotal	$26.84
Tax	$1.61
Total	$28.45
Amount Paid	$28.45
Balance Due	$0.00

Form 55

Park Department Stores

Today's Date	3/23
CHILD'S JACKET Item #12114	$22.98
CHILD'S JEANS Item #12830	$14.29
CHILD'S T-SHIRT Item #12872	$ 9.99
CHILD'S PANTS Item #12661	$13.55
SUBTOTAL	$60.81
6% TAX	$ 3.65
TOTAL	$64.46
PAID	$64.46

Refunds & Exchanges Require Receipt

Form 56

BURGER EXPRESS

```
KID'S MEAL..... 3.99
BURGER......... 3.29
SM FRIES.......  .99
SM DRINK.......  .99

SUB............ 9.26
TAX............  .56
TOT............ 9.82
PAID...........10.00
CHG............  .18
```

THANK YOU

Customer Name:	Adam G. Warner
Customer Card #:	0000 4321 0000 9867

Date Due:	3/31/--
Balance:	$133.45
Minimum Payment:	$ 10.00
Payment Enclosed:	________

WorldCard

WorldCard
Box 5800
Carlton MO 63011

RETURN THIS PORTION WITH YOUR PAYMENT.

Tori Davis-Martinez — Account No. 0000 4321 0000 9867

Date	Description	Reference Number	Amount
3/6	GasCo	75420TR	$ 35.24
3/12	GasCo	69998BC	$ 34.41
3/18	Books Etc. (www.booksetc.com)	29666SR	$ 29.95
3/21	GasCo	42325DK	$ 33.85
		Total	$133.45

WorldCard

For Customer Service, call 555-555-7422

Form 59

THANK YOU FOR SHOPPING
HILLTOP GROCERY STORE

DAVID WAS YOUR CASHIER.
DATE 3/27 TIME 6:11

CHICKEN BREASTS	4.12
0.96 LB @ 4.29/LB	
SHAMPOO*	3.45
ALUM FOIL*	2.75
COOKIES	3.29
GALA APPLES	1.20
1.04 LB @ 1.15/LB	
TOILET PAPER*	3.77
BAGELS	3.96
4 @ .99	
SUBTOTAL	$85.04
*TAX	$ 2.10
TOTAL	$87.14
DEBIT	$87.14

Form 58

GasCo

Date: 3/27
Station: 618
Pump: 1

Regular Gas $33.27

Charged to WorldCard **** 9867

Save this receipt for your records.

Form 60

Trent County Auto Mall (937) 555–AUTO

BILL OF SALE

Salesperson: Bob Chen   Date: 3/29/--

Customer: Adam G. Warner

Address: 4412 Lincoln Ave Hopewell, OH 45313

Home Phone: 937-555-2262   Bus. Phone: 937-555-3777

Trade-In

Make: Meridian   Model: Se Sedan   Mileage: 98,678

Car Purchased ☐ New ☒ Used

Make: Olympic   Model: S-Class Sedan   Mileage: 11,081

Features

- ☐ Manual Transmission
- ☒ Automatic Transmission
- ☒ Anti-lock Brakes
- ☒ Driver-side Air Bag
- ☒ Passenger Air Bag
- ☒ Air Conditioning
- ☐ Standard Sound System
- ☒ Deluxe Sound System
- ☒ Power Windows
- ☒ Power Locks
- ☐ Sun Roof
- ☒ Floor Mats

List Price	16,500	00
Purchase Price	15,200	00
Document Fees	40	00
Subtotal	15,240	00
6% Sales Tax	914	40
State & Local Fees	155	25
Total Price	16,309	65
Trade-in Allowance	1,700	00
Partial Payment	3,600	00
Balance	11,009	65

Bob Chen
DEALER'S SIGNATURE

Adam G. Warner
CUSTOMER SIGNATURE

3/29/--
DATE

Financing   Bank: Hopewell Community Bank

Amount: $11,009.65   Loan Approval #: 21-339214

Form 61

Bit-Zee Booksellers
Hopewell Pavilion

Storybook Item 5445-57254	$7.00
Picture Book Item 4520-64111	$10.50

Subtotal	$17.50
Sales Tax 6%	$ 1.05
Total	$18.55
Payment by check Amount of check	$18.55

Ask about Bit-Zee Reading Rewards

Hopewell Community Bank

Adam G. Warner
4412 Lincoln Ave
Hopewell, OH 45313

Statement prepared on:	3/27/--
Opening Balance:	$639.27
Closing Balance:	$1,290.40
Account Number:	21-436587

Checks

Check No.	Date Paid	Amount
672	3/5	54.78
673	3/6	900.00
674	3/11	201.40
675	3/19	620.00
676	3/21	73.00

Check No.	Date Paid	Amount
677	3/23	25.00
678	3/22	20.00
679	3/25	222.60
680	3/26	28.45
681	3/27	64.46

Debits and Withdrawals

Date	Amount	Description
3/4	105.10	Online payment: Hopewell Energy, Inc.
3/4	34.31	Online payment: PBC Telephone Co
3/4	136.95	Online payment: Express Cable Service
3/6	79.33	Debit transaction: Hilltop Grocery
3/14	70.49	Debit transaction: Hilltop Grocery
3/22	92.14	Debit transaction: Hilltop Grocery
3/27	87.14	Debit transaction: Hilltop Grocery
3/27	10.00	Service Charge: Online Bill Payment Service

Deposits

Date	Amount	Description
3/2	1,737.51	Direct Payroll Deposit: Cabot Services
3/17	1,737.51	Direct Payroll Deposit: Cabot Services
3/27	1.26	Interest Earned

Form 62

HOPEWELL COMMUNITY BANK

Account Reconciliation Form

1. Enter closing balance from statement. $________

2. List deposits/credits made after statement date:

DATE	AMOUNT	DATE	AMOUNT	DATE	AMOUNT

Enter total of above deposits and credits. $________

3. Compute subtotal (#1 plus #2). $________

4. List checks, withdrawals, and debits not yet paid by bank:

CHECK NO. OR DATE	AMOUNT	CHECK NO. OR DATE	AMOUNT	CHECK NO. OR DATE	AMOUNT

Enter total of above checks, withdrawals, and debits. $________

5. Enter revised bank balance (#3 minus #4). $________

6. Enter checkbook balance $______
   Subtract service charges $______
   Add interest paid $______
   Enter result $________

Final amount on Line 6 should be the same as your revised bank balance on Line 5. If not, please consult section below.

If revised bank balance is MORE than your checkbook balance:	If revised bank balance is LESS than your checkbook balance:
(a) Have you checked your addition and subtraction above and in your checkbook?	(a) Have you checked your addition and subtraction above and in your checkbook?
(b) Does the above list include all of your outstanding checks, withdrawals, and debits?	(b) Have you deducted service and other bank charges in your checkbook?
(c) Have you added all ATM deposits in your checkbook?	c) Have you deducted all ATM withdrawals in your checkbook?
(d) Have you added all credits and advances in your checkbook?	(d) Have you deducted all credit line and preauthorized payments in your checkbook?

In case of errors or questions about your account, call (937) 555-6000.

Form 63

STATEMENT OF NET WORTH FOR ____________________

Assets

Checking Account	
Savings Account	
CDs	
Home	
Cars	
Personal Items	
Cash	
Total Assets	

Liabilities and Net Worth

Liabilities and Net Worth	Amount
Mortgage	
Phone Bill	
Gas/Electric Bill	
Internet Service Bill	
Satellite TV Bill	
Car Loans	
Home Insurance	
Car Registration	
Income Tax	
Property Tax	
Total Liabilities	
Net Worth	
Total Liabilities and Net Worth	

Form 64

BUDGET WORKSHEET FOR ____________________

Monthly Income

Gross Pay .... ________
Taxes/Deductions .... ________
Net Pay .... ________

Monthly Expenses

Savings/Debt Payoff .... ________
Savings Accounts .... ________
Investments .... ________
Loan Payments .... ________
Other (________) ________

Home .... ________
Rent/Mortgage Payment .... ________
Property Taxes .... ________
Utilities .... ________
Phone/Pager Service .... ________
Cable/Satellite TV Service .... ________
Internet Service .... ________
Home Maintenance .... ________
Home/Renter's Insurance .... ________
Home Furnishings .... ________
Home Electronics .... ________

Food/Sundries .... ________
Food .... ________
Personal Care Items .... ________
Small Home Care Items .... ________

Personal .... ________
Clothes & Shoes .... ________
Haircuts/Salon Services .... ________
Dry Cleaning/Laundry .... ________
Gym Membership .... ________
Life Insurance .... ________

Column 1 Total .... ________

Transportation .... ________
Car Loan Payment .... ________
Car Insurance .... ________
Gasoline/Oil .... ________
Car Maintenance .... ________
License/Registration Fees .... ________
Bus/Subway Fares .... ________

Entertainment .... ________
Restaurant Meals .... ________
Event Fees/Tickets .... ________
Travel Expenses .... ________

Miscellaneous .... ________
Child Care Expenses .... ________
Gifts .... ________
Donations/Charities .... ________
Pet/Hobby Expenses .... ________
Education Fees .... ________
Bank Service Charges .... ________

Health Care .... ________
Doctor & Dental Fees .... ________
Prescription Medicines .... ________
Glasses/Contact Lenses .... ________

Column 2 Total .... ________
Grand Total .... ________

Form 65

Remit to:

Lancaster State Bank
PO Box 19622
Maplewood OH 44921

MORTGAGE PAYMENT

Jared and Celina Hoffman
363 Sherwood Circle
Maplewood, OH 44922

Date Due: 4/8/20--
Amount Due: $830.00
Loan Number: 622 0987

Form 66

Capital
Service Station

DATE: 4/2
TIME: 5:21 pm
STATION #: 324

REGULAR	$35.25
TOTAL DUE	$35.25
DEBIT CARD PYMT	$35.25
CHANGE DUE	$00.00

Form 67

Thank You for Shopping
FAMILY FOODS

DATE: 4/2 TIME: 6:08

SALAD BAR	2.72
FROZEN JUICE	1.19
FROZEN JUICE	1.19
DELI	2.39
BAKERY	1.98
BANANAS	
1.55 LB @ .59/LB	.91
SUBTOTAL	95.69
TAX*	2.25
TOTAL	97.94
DEBIT PYMT	97.94

Form 69

WATER POINT GRILLE

Date: April 04,20– –

SERVER: CHEYANNE

LEMONADE	3.00
GRILLED TUNA	26.00
ICED TEA	2.50
PASTA W SHRIMP	21.00
MINERAL WATER	4.00
SEA SCALLOPS	25.00
SOFT DRINK	2.50
CHICKEN PICCATA	18.00
SUBTOTAL	102.00
TAX	6.12
TOTAL	108.12

Thank You

Form 68

REGALO
Gifts and Candles

Candle holder #096 3241	26.00
9" pillar #005 8724	8.50
Subtotal	34.50
Tax	2.07
Total Due	36.57
Paid by Check	36.57

20-- Estimated Tax Worksheet

Keep for Your Records

1	Adjusted gross income you expect in 20-- (see instructions)	1	
2	• If you plan to itemize deductions, enter the estimated total of your itemized deductions. **Caution:** *If line 1 above is over $159,950 ($79,975 if married filing separately), your deduction may be reduced. See Pub. 505 for details.* • If you do not plan to itemize deductions, enter your standard deduction from page 1.	2	
3	Subtract line 2 from line 1	3	
4	Exemptions. Multiply $3,500 by the number of personal exemptions. **Caution:** *See Pub. 505 to figure the amount to enter if line 1 above is over: $239,950 if married filing jointly or qualifying widow(er); $199,950 if head of household; $159,950 if single; or $119,975 if married filing separately*	4	
5	Subtract line 4 from line 3	5	
6	**Tax.** Figure your tax on the amount on line 5 by using the **20-- Tax Rate Schedules** on page 5. **Caution:** *If you will have qualified dividends or a net capital gain, or expect to claim the foreign earned income exclusion or housing exclusion, see Pub. 505 to figure the tax*	6	
7	Alternative minimum tax from **Form 6251**	7	
8	Add lines 6 and 7. Add to this amount any other taxes you expect to include in the total on Form 1040, line 44, or Form 1040A, line 28	8	
9	Credits (see instructions below). **Do not** include any income tax withholding on this line	9	
10	Subtract line 9 from line 8. If zero or less, enter -0-	10	
11	Self-employment tax (see instructions below). Estimate of 20-- net earnings from self-employment $____________ ; if **$102,000 or less,** multiply the amount by 15.3%; if **more than $102,000,** multiply the amount by 2.9%, add $12,648 to the result, and enter the total. **Caution:** *If you also have wages subject to social security tax, see Pub. 505 to figure the amount to enter*	11	
12	Other taxes (see instructions below)	12	
13a	Add lines 10 through 12	13a	
b	Earned income credit, additional child tax credit, and credits from **Forms 4136, 8801 (line 27),** and **8885**	13b	
c	**Total 20-- estimated tax.** Subtract line 13b from line 13a. If zero or less, enter -0- ▶	13c	
14a	Multiply line 13c by 90% (66⅔ % for farmers and fishermen) — 14a		
b	Enter the tax shown on your 20-- tax return (110% of that amount if you are not a farmer or fisherman and the adjusted gross income shown on that return is more than $150,000 or, if married filing separately for 20--, more than $75,000) — 14b		
c	**Required annual payment to avoid a penalty.** Enter the **smaller** of line 14a or 14b ▶ **Caution:** *Generally, if you do not prepay (through income tax withholding and estimated tax payments) at least the amount on line 14c, you may owe a penalty for not paying enough estimated tax. To avoid a penalty, make sure your estimate on line 13c is as accurate as possible. Even if you pay the required annual payment, you may still owe tax when you file your return. If you prefer, you can pay the amount shown on line 13c. For details, see Pub. 505.*	14c	
15	Income tax withheld and estimated to be withheld during 20-- (including income tax withholding on pensions, annuities, certain deferred income, etc.)	15	
16a	Subtract line 15 from line 14c — 16a Is the result zero or less? ☐ **Yes.** Stop here. You are not required to make estimated tax payments. ☐ **No.** Go to line 16b.		
b	Subtract line 15 from line 13c — 16b Is the result less than $1,000? ☐ **Yes.** Stop here. You are not required to make estimated tax payments. ☐ **No.** Go to line 17 to figure your required payment.		
17	If the first payment you are required to make is due April 15, 20--, enter ¼ of line 16a (minus any 20-- overpayment that you are applying to this installment) here, and on your estimated tax payment voucher(s) if you are paying by check or money order. (**Note:** *Household employers, see instructions below.)*	17	

Form 71

Sumida's
LAWN & GARDEN

DATE: APRIL 07,20 – –

MULCH	32.90
10 @ 3.29	
GARDEN HOSE	22.98
NOZZLE	12.50
SUBTOTAL	68.38
TAX	4.10
TOTAL	72.48

THANK YOU

Form 72

Thank You for Shopping
FAMILY FOODS

DATE: 4/8 TIME: 2:56

PORK CHOPS	
1.25 LB @ 4.25/LB	5.31
BREAD	2.25
MILK	2.49
BAGELS	1.29
CEREAL	4.25
SUBTOTAL	70.43
TAX*	1.89
TOTAL	72.32
DEBIT PYMT	72.32

Celina and Jared Hoffman
363 Sherwood Circle
Maplewood, OH 44922

Universal Cellular

Account No.: 419-555-9113

Amount Due by 4/14/--: $87.40

Universal Cellular, Inc.
Dept. 2510
South Bay, CA 94199

Save this portion for your records.

Primary Phone (419) 555-9113

Basic Plus text and long distance 49.00

Tax 7.35

Additional Phone(419) 555-9178

Basic service 27.00

Tax 4.05

Total 87.40

Universal Cellular

Your Global Connection

Form 74

Jared and Celina Hoffman
363 Sherwood Circle
Maplewood, OH 44922

Acct. No.	621-BT
Amount Due	$112.28
Date Due	4/16/--

TCG&E

Tri-County Gas & Electric
P.O. Box 13579
Maplewood, OH 44920

Detach and return this portion with your payment.

BILLING EXPLANATION

BILLING PERIOD	ITEM	CURRENT CHARGES
3/1 – 3/31	Gas Meter #2216	$36.12
	Electricity Meter #55319M	$76.16

Questions? Please call 419-555-4679 for service.

TRI-COUNTY GAS & ELECTRIC

TDS Satellite TV

Amount Due: $49.82
Due Date: 4/15/20--

Account No.: 3XTS696

Celina and Jared Hoffman
363 Sherwood Circle
Maplewood, OH 44922

TDS Satellite TV
2222 Newton Boulevard
Waycross, OR 97297

Keep this statement for your records.

Top Choice Basic with Local Channels $47.00

Sales Tax 2.82

Total $49.82

For service from 3/1/-- to 3/31/20--.

Account No.: 3XTS696

Upgrade to premium service NOW, and receive 5 pay-per-view movies FREE!

TDS Satellite TV

Form 76

Delores Cruz-Smith CFP

Certified Financial Planner **(419) 555-6820**

28 Lexington Ave., Suite C
Maplewood, OH 44920

Client Name *Celina and Jared Hoffman*

Service Provided *Financial assessment & advice*

Date *4/10/--*

Amount *$390.00* **Paid By** *Check*

Signature *Delores Cruz-Smith*

Form 77

Capital
Service Station

DATE: 4/11
TIME: 9:26 pm
STATION #: 324

REGULAR	$34.11
TOTAL DUE	$34.11
DEBIT CARD PYMT	$34.11
CHANGE DUE	$00.00

State of Ohio

VEHICLE REGISTRATION EXPIRATION NOTICE

Amount Due: $55.00

Celina Hoffman
363 Sherwood Circle
Maplewood, OH 44922

Vehicle Plate No.	PKX 703
Plate Category	Passenger
Vehicle Type	4S
Year	2007
VIN	2PSTOX5822RL08917
County	Grant

YOUR VEHICLE REGISTRATION EXPIRES ON: 4/20/--

Make checks payable to the Ohio Department of Motor Vehicles.

Return this portion with your check or money order.

Name: Keisha Booker
SSN: 912-65-0018

Fees:	License Fee	**$49.00**
	Service Charge	**$6.00**
Total Amount Due:		**$55.00**

Date Due: 4/20/--

Ohio Dept. of Motor Vehicles
P.O. Box 721
Columbus, OH 43216

Maplewood Medical Center

Employee 401(k) Enrollment Form

PARTICIPANT INFORMATION

Participant Name:____________________ Date of Birth: __________

Social Security Number: ____________________ Marital Status: __________

CONTRIBUTIONS

1. Choose the percentage of your earnings you wish to contribute. Circle only one.
   1% 2% 3% 4% 5% 6% 7% 8% 9% 10%

INVESTMENT INFORMATION

2. Indicate the percentage of your contribution you wish to contribute to each of the options listed below. Use 10% increments.

   Government Money Trust __________%

   Government Intermediate Fund __________%

   Balanced Mutual Fund __________%

   Blue Chip Fund __________%

   International Fund __________%

   Aggressive Growth Fund __________%

   TOTAL (Your choices must total 100%.) __________%

BENEFICIARY INFORMATION

3. Primary Beneficiary: __________%
   Name: ________________
   Relationship : ________________

   Primary Beneficiary: __________%
   Name: ________________
   Relationship: ________________

4. Secondary Beneficiary: __________%
   Name : ________________
   Relationship: ________________

   Secondary Beneficiary: __________%
   Name: ________________
   Relationship: ________________

SIGNATURE

Participant Signature: ________________ Date: ________________

Form 80

Thank You for Shopping
FAMILY FOODS

DATE: 4/14 TIME: 5:41

COFFEE	6.49
PASTA	1.29
CHICKEN 1.08 LB @ 4.19/LB	4.53
COOKIES	2.85
CHEESE	4.47
FLOUR	2.19
SUBTOTAL	81.77
TAX*	2.94
TOTAL	84.71
DEBIT PYMT	84.71

Form 81

From: autoconfirm@pilotnet.com

Sent: April 14, 20—

To: celhoff22@pilotnet.com

Subject: Payment Confirmation

Dear Pilot customer,

Your credit card has been charged this month's Internet connection fee.

Amount: $41.34

For: March 14-April 14, 20--

Charged to: WorldCard # ****0908

Customer:
Celina Hoffman
363 Sherwood Circle
Maplewood, OH 44922
Email: celhoff22@pilotnet.com

From:
Pilot Internet Connections
665 Wellfleet Plaza
San Francisco, CA 94101

For help in using our service, please visit our online customer support at www.pilotnet.com/support. To view your account details, please log onto your account from our home page www.pilotnet.com. For billing questions, you may contact us by email at customersupport@pilotnet.com, or call 1-800-555-9000.

Thank you for choosing Pilot Internet Connections!

Form 82

Goldberg's Hardware

PAINT	2 @ 18.67	37.34
TRIM PAINT		20.86
BRUSH		9.85
ROLLER KIT		13.17
SUB		81.22
TAX		4.87
AMT OWED		86.09
AMT PAID		86.09

Form 83

Jared and Celina Hoffman
363 Sherwood Circle
Maplewood, OH 44922

PaxCo
INSURANCE

Amount Due: $47.50
Date Due: 4/20/--
Account No.: 447–OHG

PaxCo Insurance Co.
280 Mesa Blvd.
Los Angeles, CA 90064

Retain this statement for your records.

Coverage Period	*Insurance Type*	*Amount*
5/1 to 5/31	Standard Homeowner's Coverage	$47.50
	Total	**$47.50**

PaxCo
INSURANCE

Due Date **4/20/--**

Form 84

Comfort First Uniforms

DATE: April 18, 20 – –

One-pocket, V-neck, blue, XL	$ 14.99
One-pocket, V-neck, blue, XL	14.99
One-pocket, V-neck, blue, XL	0.00
>>Buy two get one free	
Drawstring pants, blue, M-tall	18.99
Drawstring pants, blue, M-tall	18.99
Drawstring pants, blue, M-tall	0.00
>>Buy two get one free	
SUBTOTAL	$67.96
TAX	4.08
TOTAL	$72.04

Thank You

Form 85

Thank You for Shopping
FAMILY FOODS

DATE: 4/21 TIME: 5:23

ICE CREAM	4.27
RICE MIX	1.96
MILK	1.59
ORANGES 3/1.50	3.00
LETTUCE .72 LB @ 1.74/LB	1.25
SUBTOTAL	$65.13
TAX*	$ 2.69
TOTAL	$67.82
DEBIT PYMT	$67.82

Form 86

Capital
Service Station

DATE: 4/21
TIME: 6:15 pm
STATION #: 324

REGULAR	$32.72
TOTAL DUE	$32.72
CASH PYMT	$40.00
CHANGE DUE	$ 7.28

Form 87

Lancaster State Bank

Automated Teller Machine

Date: 4/24
Time: 6:12 pm
Checking Account #: 334-067214
Withdrawal Amount: $200.00

Form 88

The Bistro

Date: April 24, 20 - -

SERVER MARVIN	
SOUP DE JOUR CUP	3.75
PORTEBELLA SANDWICH	9.50
W FRESH FRUIT	0.00
DIET COLA	2.50
HOUSE SALAD	4.50
VINIGRETTE ON SIDE	0.00
GRILLED CHICKEN	21.75
W RICE PILAF	0.00
ICED TEA	2.50
SUBTOTAL	$44.50
TAX	2.67
TOTAL	$47.17
CASH PAID	$50.00
CHANGE	$ 2.83

Form 89

Hopewell Playhouse
presents
Comedy of Errors

Ticket Price: $35.00
Service Fee: $2.50 Total Price: $37.50

SEAT D 16

Hopewell Playhouse
presents
Comedy of Errors

Ticket Price: $35.00
Service Fee: $2.50 Total Price: $37.50

SEAT D 15

Form 90

Daniel K. Murad, D.O.
118 Medical Center Dr.
Maplewood, OH 44919
(419) 555-5652

Maplewood Optometry Associates

DATE	PATIENT NAME	SERVICE	FEE
4/25/--	Jared Hoffman	Annual exam	$93.00
		TOTAL FEE	$93.00
		PATIENT COPAY.	$30.00
		INSURER'S COPAY.	$63.00

Form 91

Remit to:

LANCASTER STATE BANK
PO Box 19622
Maplewood, OH 44921

CAR LOAN PAYMENT

Jared and Celina Hoffman
363 Sherwood Circle
Maplewood, OH 44922

Date Due: 4/29/--
Amount Due: $216.40
Loan Account Number: 1318-1163

Form 92

Jared and Celina Hoffman	Due Date	4/29/--
363 Sherwood Circle	Amount	$240.60
Maplewood, OH 44922	Car Loan I.D.#	0-14967-822

Oak Grove Bank

1502 Whitehurst Ave.
Maplewood, OH 44920

Form 93

CHANDLER$_x$

Date: April 27, 20 – –

Deodorant, 3.25 oz	2.99
Shampoo, 8.45 fl oz	7.47
Razor Refill Cartridges, 8 ct	16.99
Dental Floss, 100 yards	6.99
Contact Solution, 24 fl oz	19.99
SUBTOTAL:	54.43
TAX:	3.27
TOTAL:	57.70

Please Come Again!

Grant County

Office of Property Taxes

Owners: Jared and Celina Hoffman

Property: 363 Sherwood Circle
Maplewood, OH 44922

Tax Period: July 1 to December 31, 20 - -

Tax Amount: $1,650.00

Tax Due: 5/5/--

Make your check or money order payable to:

Grant County Treasurer

Thank you.

Return this statement with your check or money order.

Jared and Celina Hoffman
363 Sherwood Circle
Maplewood, OH 44922

Property tax due: $1,650.00
Date due: 5/5/--

Grant County Treasurer
Box 2000
Maplewood, OH 44920

Lancaster State Bank

HOME LOAN QUALIFYING APPLICATION

APPLICANT INFORMATION

APPLICANT	CO-APPLICANT
Name ______	Name ______
Address ______	Address ______
______	______
Home Ph ______ Work Ph ______	Home Ph ______ Work Ph ______
SSN ______ Age ______	SSN ______ Age ______
Employer ______	Employer ______
Employer's Address ______	Employer's Address ______
Title/Position ______	Title/Position ______
Years with Current Employer ______	Years with Current Employer ______

INCOME INFORMATION

	APPLICANT	CO-APPLICANT
Base Employment Income	______	______
Overtime	______	______
Commissions	______	______
Rental Income	______	______
TOTAL	______	______

ASSETS

Checking Account	______
Savings Account	______
Retirement Accounts	______
CDs/Money Markets	______
Other Investments	______
Non-liquid Assets (cars, personal items, house)	______

LIABILITIES

	MONTHLY PAYMENT
Mortgage Payment	______
Credit Card Debt	______
Alimony	______
Child Care/Support	______
Other Loans	______

APPLICANT SIGNATURE & DATE ______________________

CO-APPLICANT SIGNATURE & DATE ______________________

Form 96

Lancaster State Bank

Celina and Jared Hoffman
363 Sherwood Circle
Maplewood, OH 44922

Statement prepared on:	4/28/20--
Opening Balance:	$6,922.82
Closing Balance:	$3,148.58
Account Number:	334-067214

Checks

Check No.	Date Paid	Amount
1312	4/4	830.00
1313	4/5	36.57
1314	4/9	2,492.00
1315	4/9	72.48
1316	4/13	390.00
1317	4/15	55.00

Check No.	Date Paid	Amount
1318	4/19	420.00
1319	4/18	86.09
1320	4/21	47.50
1321	4/21	72.04
1322	4/25	1,500.00
1323	4/28	30.00

Debits and Withdrawals

Date	Amount	Description
4/2	35.25	Debit transaction: Capital Service Station
4/2	97.94	Debit transaction: Family Foods
4/8	72.32	Debit transaction: Family Foods
4/9	87.40	Online payment: Universal Cellular
4/9	112.28	Online payment: Tri-County Gas & Electric
4/9	49.82	Online payment: TDS Satellite TV
4/11	34.11	Debit transaction: Capital Service Station
4/14	84.71	Debit transaction: Family Foods
4/21	67.82	Debit transaction: Family Foods
4/24	200.00	ATM Withdrawal
4/28	7.00	Service Charge: Online Bill Payment Service

Deposits

Date	Amount	Description
4/15	1,606.09	Direct Deposit: Maplewood Medical Center
4/20	1,500.00	Deposit

Form 96

Account Reconciliation Form

1. Enter closing balance from statement. $________

2. List deposits/credits made after statement date:

DATE	AMOUNT	DATE	AMOUNT	DATE	AMOUNT

Enter total of above deposits and credits. $________

3. Compute subtotal (#1 plus #2). $________

4. List checks, withdrawals, and debits not yet paid by bank:

CHECK NO. OR DATE	AMOUNT	CHECK NO. OR DATE	AMOUNT	CHECK NO. OR DATE	AMOUNT

Enter total of above checks, withdrawals, and debits. $________

5. Enter revised bank balance (#3 minus #4). $________

6. Enter checkbook balance $________
   Subtract service charges $________
   Add interest paid $________
   Enter result $________

Final amount on Line 6 should be the same as your revised bank balance on Line 5. If not, please consult section below.

If revised bank balance is MORE than your checkbook balance:	If revised bank balance is LESS than your checkbook balance:
(a) Have you checked your addition and subtraction above and in your checkbook?	(a) Have you checked your addition and subtraction above and in your checkbook?
(b) Does the above list include all of your outstanding checks, withdrawals, and debits?	(b) Have you deducted service and other bank charges in your checkbook?
(c) Have you added all ATM deposits in your checkbook?	c) Have you deducted all ATM withdrawals in your checkbook?
(d) Have you added all credits and advances in your checkbook?	(d) Have you deducted all credit line and preauthorized payments in your checkbook?

assets cash and anything of value that you own

automated teller machine (ATM) bank computer that allows you to make transactions, such as deposits and withdrawals, without actually going inside the bank

automatic bill payment making ongoing bill payments by granting the company the authority to charge the amount to your credit card or deduct it from your bank account at stated intervals, such as monthly, without sending you a bill first; the transactions appear on your bank or credit card statements

average a "typical" number in a set of numbers, calculated by adding the numbers in the set and dividing the sum by the number of numbers in the set; for example, the average of 32, 33, and 34 is 32 + 33 + 34 = 99, divided by 3, which equals 33

bonds investments in corporations or governments that represent loans that these organizations must repay by a specified date

budget plan for dividing up your income among saving and spending options

canceled checks checks that have been processed through the banking system and the amounts have been subtracted from your checking account

certificate of deposit (CD) deposit in a savings institution that earns a stated interest rate for a specific period of time

certified financial planners investment professionals who help their clients achieve their financial goals through sound planning and investing

checkbook register form for recording all deposits to and withdrawals from your checking account, including written checks and electronic transactions

claims requests made to an insurance company to pay the amount due under the terms of the policy

copayment under certain health care plans, such as an HMO or PPO, the portion of the total medical fee or prescription cost that the patient pays

credit agreement to borrow money now and repay it later, usually with monthly payments

credit line maximum amount of unpaid debt allowed on the account

debit card bank card that you can use like a check to pay for purchases at a store or make transactions on your account using an automated teller machine

dependent for tax purposes, someone who relies on someone else for financial support

direct deposit method of payment in which funds are deposited directly into the payee's bank account; often used for paychecks and tax refunds

diversify distributing funds among a variety of investments to reduce the overall risk; for example, mutual funds diversify by pooling the funds of many individual investors to purchases the stocks and bonds of a wide variety of organizations

dividends part of a corporation's profits paid out to its stockholders

down payment the first, typically large, payment on an expensive item made at the time of purchase

estimate written document, provided before work begins, showing how much the service is likely to cost

exemptions deductions from taxable income allowed by the IRS

finance charge any fee for the use of credit; could include a monthly fee for use of a credit card, interest, and other fees

finances money and other resources

401(k) account tax-deferred retirement savings plan offered to employees by their employer

franchise one of a chain of individually owned businesses authorized to sell the chain's products; for example, McDonald's restaurants are owned by different people but they all sell McDonald's products

fringe benefits any compensation other than wages that you receive from you employer, such as paid vacation time and paid life insurance.

gross pay total earned before taxes and other deductions have been subtracted

health maintenance organization (HMO) corporation made up of doctors and other health professionals who provide a range of health care services to employee groups for a set monthly rate

homeowner's insurance insurance that pays part of the cost of replacing stolen possessions and repairing damage to the owner's house caused by fire, storms, or other hazards

individual retirement account (IRA) tax-deferred investment account for people who do not participate in a retirement plan through their employer

installments payments made at regular intervals to pay off a large debt

interest fee for using borrowed money, usually expressed as a rate, or percentage of the unpaid balance

investing allowing others to use your extra money to conduct their business, in exchange for which you earn interest

liabilities money owed

life insurance insurance that pays a stated amount to a named person if the insured person dies

money market account savings account whose funds are invested in safe types of securities; the interest rate goes up and down a small amount as the values of the securities change

mortgage home loan

mutual fund a collection of stocks and bonds purchased by a professional fund manager with a pool of money from many investors

net pay amount of money you take home after taxes and other deductions have been removed

net worth dollar value of all the things you own, minus the sum of your debts

outstanding check check that has not finished its processing route from the payee's bank back to yours, so your bank has not yet subtracted the amount from your account

paycheck stub attachment to your paycheck that shows how much you earned and how much money was deducted for taxes, health insurance, etc.

payee person or business to whom the check is written

payment voucher form mailed with a check to identify what the check is to be used for

personal identification number (PIN) your "secret code" that allows you, and no one else, to use your account

preferred provider organization (PPO) network of doctors and health facilities that have contracted with employers to offer health services to their employees

premium regular payment required to purchase insurance

prove cash to total and verify the transactions in your financial record

quotation written description of the terms and price of something you wish to buy, such as an insurance policy

real estate land and any buildings on it

reconcile a checkbook to make sure that your record of checking account transactions matches your bank's records

refinance take out a new loan to pay off an existing loan, usually to get a lower interest rate

refund for income taxes, the excess amount of money returned to you if too much tax was withheld from your paychecks during the year

renter's insurance type of home insurance that covers personal property in a rented residence in case of loss from fire, storms, theft, or other hazards

risk (investment) chance that your investment may lose value, resulting in loss of interest or even loss of the money you invested

roll over to reinvest money in the same or similar account

Roth IRA retirement account in which you pay income taxes on your contributions but do not pay taxes when you withdraw the money at retirement; as a result, the account's earnings are tax-free

self-employed working for yourself, running your own business

service charge fee charged by a bank for performing services for you; for example, a bank may deduct a service charge from your account for processing each check your write and for use of the automated teller machines

shares of stock units of ownership in a corporation

stockholders investors who are part-owners a corporation because they own shares of its stock

sundries small personal and home care items typically found in a grocery or drug store, such as shampoo, light bulbs, toilet paper, etc.

taxable income total income on which you must pay tax

tax credits amounts you may subtract from the tax you owe

tax-deferred income income on which taxes are put off until a later date, such as retirement age

term life insurance life insurance policy that pays a stated amount if the insured person dies within the time period stated in the policy; unlike other kinds of life insurance, term policies have no savings component

transaction event that involves money coming in or going out

utilities essential services, such as gas and electricity, water, and garbage collection, often provided by government-regulated companies

void a check destroy a check by writing the word "VOID" in large letters across it to so that no one can cash it

withholding amounts that employers subtract from employees' paychecks and send to the government as payments on the employees' income taxes

Financial Record Categories

Savings/Debt Payoff
Savings Accounts
Investments
Loan Payments

Home
Rent/Mortgage Payment
Property Taxes
Utilities (gas, electric, water, etc.)
Phone/Pager Services
Cable/Satellite TV Service
Internet Service
Home Maintenance
Home/Renter's Insurance
Home Furnishings (furniture, appliances, dishes, towels, etc.)
Home Electronics (TV, computer, game system, etc.)

Food/Sundries
Food (prepared and eaten at home)
Personal Care Items (shampoo, soap, toothpaste, etc.)
Small Home Care Items (light bulbs, dishwashing liquid, etc.)

Personal
Clothes & Shoes
Haircuts/Salon Services
Dry Cleaning/Laundry
Gym Membership
Life Insurance

Transportation
Car Loan Payment
Car Insurance
Gasoline/Oil
Car Maintenance (oil change, tires, car washes, etc.)
License/Registration Fees
Bus/Subway Fares

Entertainment
Restaurant Meals (meals, snacks, and beverages; sit-down, take-out, drive-thru, etc.)
Event Fees/Tickets (movies, sporting events, etc.)
Travel Expenses (campgrounds, motels, hotels, airline tickets, rental cars, etc.)

Miscellaneous
Child Care Expenses
Gifts
Donations/Charities
Pet/Hobby Expenses
Education Fees
Bank Service Charges

Health Care
Doctor & Dental Fees
Prescription Medicines
Glasses/Contact Lenses

Part 2

	Date	Description	Deposit	Savings/Debt Payoff	Home	Food/Sundries	Personal	Transportation	Entertainment	Miscellaneous	Health Care	Balance
1												
2												
3												
4												
5												
6												
7												
8												
9												
10												
11												
12												
13												
14												
15												
16												
17												
18												
19												
20												
21												
22												
		TOTALS										

Part 2

	Date	Description	Deposit	Savings/Debt Payoff	Home	Food/Sundries	Personal	Transportation	Entertainment	Miscellaneous	Health Care	**Balance**
1												
2												
3												
4												
5												
6												
7												
8												
9												
10												
11												
12												
13												
14												
15												
16												
17												
18												
19												
20												
21												
22												
		TOTALS										

	Date	Description	Deposit	Savings/Debt Payoff	Home	Food/Sundries	Personal	Transportation	Entertainment	Miscellaneous	Health Care	**Balance**
1												
2												
3												
4												
5												
6												
7												
8												
9												
10												
11												
12												
13												
14												
15												
16												
17												
18												
19												
20												
21												
22												
		TOTALS										

	Date	Description	Deposit	Savings/Debt Payoff	Home	Food/Sundries	Personal	Transportation	Entertainment	Miscellaneous	Health Care	**Balance**
1												
2												
3												
4												
5												
6												
7												
8												
9												
10												
11												
12												
13												
14												
15												
16												
17												
18												
19												
20												
21												
22												
		TOTALS										

	Date	Description	Deposit	Savings/Debt Payoff	Home	Food/Sundries	Personal	Transportation	Entertainment	Miscellaneous	Health Care	Balance
1												
2												
3												
4												
5												
6												
7												
8												
9												
10												
11												
12												
13												
14												
15												
16												
17												
18												
19												
20												
21												
22												
		TOTALS										

	Date	Description	Deposit	Savings/Debt Payoff	Home	Food/Sundries	Personal	Transportation	Entertainment	Miscellaneous	Health Care	**Balance**
1												
2												
3												
4												
5												
6												
7												
8												
9												
10												
11												
12												
13												
14												
15												
16												
17												
18												
19												
20												
21												
22												
		TOTALS										

	Date	Description	Deposit	Savings/Debt Payoff	Home	Food/Sundries	Personal	Transportation	Entertainment	Miscellaneous	Health Care	**Balance**
1												
2												
3												
4												
5												
6												
7												
8												
9												
10												
11												
12												
13												
14												
15												
16												
17												
18												
19												
20												
21												
22												
		TOTALS										

Checkbook
with Register

Student Note

The blank checks you will need to complete Part 2 are provided in this checkbook. For the check payments in Part 3 and Part 4, you should assume the checks are already filled out for you. However, you are to record all check transactions for Parts 2, 3, and 4 in this checkbook register.

Do not detach the checkbook register pages from the checkbook.

CHECK NUMBER	DATE	DESCRIPTION OF TRANSACTION	PAYMENT/ DEBIT (−)		FEE (−)	✓	DEPOSIT/ CREDIT (+)		BALANCE FWD	
									$	
			$				$			

CHECK NUMBER	DATE	DESCRIPTION OF TRANSACTION	PAYMENT/ DEBIT (−)		FEE (−)	✓	DEPOSIT/ CREDIT (+)		BALANCE FWD	
									$	
			$				$			

CHECK NUMBER	DATE	DESCRIPTION OF TRANSACTION	PAYMENT/ DEBIT (−)		FEE (−)	✓	DEPOSIT/ CREDIT (+)		BALANCE FWD	
									$	
			$				$			

CHECK NUMBER	DATE	DESCRIPTION OF TRANSACTION	PAYMENT/ DEBIT (−)		FEE (−)	✓	DEPOSIT/ CREDIT (+)		BALANCE FWD	
									$	
			$				$			

Please List Each Check Separately

CHECKS	DOLLARS	CENTS
1		
2		
3		
4		
5		
6		
7		
8		
9		
10		
11		
12		
13		
14		
15		
16		
TOTAL THIS SIDE ENTER THIS TOTAL ON REVERSE SIDE		

Tyra M. Burns
4500 Red Maple Lane, Apt. 115
Maplewood, OH 44920

98-765/43

DATE ______________________

Checks and other items are received for deposit subject to the terms and conditions of this bank's collection agreement.

FCB First City Bank

⑆98765⑆ 12⑈345678⑈

CASH			
CHECKS Endorse and List Each Check by Bank Number			
TOTAL			

FOR CLASSROOM USE ONLY

DEPOSIT TICKET

Please List Each Check Separately

CHECKS	DOLLARS	CENTS
1		
2		
3		
4		
5		
6		
7		
8		
9		
10		
11		
12		
13		
14		
15		
16		
TOTAL THIS SIDE ENTER THIS TOTAL ON REVERSE SIDE		

Tyra M. Burns
4500 Red Maple Lane, Apt. 115
Maplewood, OH 44920

98-765/43

DATE ______________________

Checks and other items are received for deposit subject to the terms and conditions of this bank's collection agreement.

CASH			
CHECKS Endorse and List Each Check by Bank Number			
TOTAL			

FOR CLASSROOM USE ONLY

DEPOSIT TICKET

FCB First City Bank

⑆98765⑆ 12⑈345678⑈

Please List Each Check Separately

CHECKS	DOLLARS	CENTS
1		
2		
3		
4		
5		
6		
7		
8		
9		
10		
11		
12		
13		
14		
15		
16		
TOTAL THIS SIDE ENTER THIS TOTAL ON REVERSE SIDE		

Tyra M. Burns
4500 Red Maple Lane, Apt. 115
Maplewood, OH 44920

98-765/43

DATE ______________________

Checks and other items are received for deposit subject to the terms and conditions of this bank's collection agreement.

FCB First City Bank

⑆98765⑆ 12⑈345678⑈

CASH			
CHECKS Endorse and List Each Check by Bank Number			
TOTAL			

FOR CLASSROOM USE ONLY

DEPOSIT TICKET

Please List Each Check Separately

CHECKS	DOLLARS	CENTS
1		
2		
3		
4		
5		
6		
7		
8		
9		
10		
11		
12		
13		
14		
15		
16		
TOTAL THIS SIDE ENTER THIS TOTAL ON REVERSE SIDE		

Tyra M. Burns
4500 Red Maple Lane, Apt. 115
Maplewood, OH 44920

98-765/43

DATE ______________________

Checks and other items are received for deposit subject to the terms and conditions of this bank's collection agreement.

FCB **First City Bank**

⑆98765⑆ 12⑈345678⑈

CASH			
CHECKS Endorse and List Each Check by Bank Number			
TOTAL			

FOR CLASSROOM USE ONLY

DEPOSIT TICKET

ENDORSE HERE

DO NOT WRITE, STAMP OR SIGN BELOW THIS LINE

RESERVED FOR FINANCIAL INSTITUTION USE*

*FEDERAL RESERVE BOARD OF GOVERNORS REG. CC

Tyra M. Burns **115**
4500 Red Maple Lane, Apt. 115
Maplewood, OH 44920

DATE ____________ 98-765/43

PAY TO THE
ORDER OF ____________ $ ______

____________ **DOLLARS**

FCB First City Bank

MEMO ____________

⑆987654⑆ 12⑈345678⑈

FOR CLASSROOM USE ONLY

ENDORSE HERE

DO NOT WRITE, STAMP OR SIGN BELOW THIS LINE

RESERVED FOR FINANCIAL INSTITUTION USE*

*FEDERAL RESERVE BOARD OF GOVERNORS REG. CC

Tyra M. Burns 114

4500 Red Maple Lane, Apt. 115

Maplewood, OH 44920

DATE ______________ 98-765/43

PAY TO THE
ORDER OF ______________ $ ______

______________ **DOLLARS**

FCB First City Bank

MEMO ______________ ______________

⑆98765⑆ 12⑈345678⑈ FOR CLASSROOM USE ONLY

ENDORSE HERE

DO NOT WRITE, STAMP OR SIGN BELOW THIS LINE

RESERVED FOR FINANCIAL INSTITUTION USE*

*FEDERAL RESERVE BOARD OF GOVERNORS REG. CC

Tyra M. Burns **113**

4500 Red Maple Lane, Apt. 115

Maplewood, OH 44920

DATE ______________________ 98-765/43

PAY TO THE
ORDER OF ______________________________ $ __________

____ **DOLLARS**

FCB First City Bank

MEMO ______________________ ______________________

⑆987654⑆ 12⑈345678⑈

FOR CLASSROOM USE ONLY

ENDORSE HERE

DO NOT WRITE, STAMP OR SIGN BELOW THIS LINE

RESERVED FOR FINANCIAL INSTITUTION USE*

*FEDERAL RESERVE BOARD OF GOVERNORS REG. CC

Tyra M. Burns **112**

4500 Red Maple Lane, Apt. 115

Maplewood, OH 44920

DATE ____________________ 98-765/43

PAY TO THE ORDER OF ____________________________ $ __________

____ **DOLLARS**

FCB First City Bank

MEMO ____________________ ____________________

⑆987654⑆ 12⑈345678⑈ FOR CLASSROOM USE ONLY

ENDORSE HERE

DO NOT WRITE, STAMP OR SIGN BELOW THIS LINE

RESERVED FOR FINANCIAL INSTITUTION USE*

*FEDERAL RESERVE BOARD OF GOVERNORS REG. CC

Tyra M. Burns **111**

4500 Red Maple Lane, Apt. 115

Maplewood, OH 44920 DATE ____________ 98-765/43

PAY TO THE
ORDER OF ____________ $ ______

____________ **DOLLARS**

FCB First City Bank

MEMO ____________ ____________

⑆987651⑆ 12⑈345678⑈ FOR CLASSROOM USE ONLY

ENDORSE HERE

DO NOT WRITE, STAMP OR SIGN BELOW THIS LINE

RESERVED FOR FINANCIAL INSTITUTION USE*

*FEDERAL RESERVE BOARD OF GOVERNORS REG. CC

Tyra M. Burns **110**

4500 Red Maple Lane, Apt. 115

Maplewood, OH 44920

DATE ______________________ 98-765/43

PAY TO THE
ORDER OF ______________________ $ __________

______________________ **DOLLARS**

FCB First City Bank

MEMO ______________________ ______________________

⑆98765⑆ 12⑈345678⑈ FOR CLASSROOM USE ONLY

ENDORSE HERE

DO NOT WRITE, STAMP OR SIGN BELOW THIS LINE

RESERVED FOR FINANCIAL INSTITUTION USE*

*FEDERAL RESERVE BOARD OF GOVERNORS REG. CC

Tyra M. Burns
4500 Red Maple Lane, Apt. 115
Maplewood, OH 44920

109

DATE ____________________ 98-765/43

PAY TO THE
ORDER OF ______________________________ $ __________

____ **DOLLARS**

FCB First City Bank

MEMO ____________________ ____________________

⑆98765⑆ 12⑈345678⑈

FOR CLASSROOM USE ONLY

ENDORSE HERE

DO NOT WRITE, STAMP OR SIGN BELOW THIS LINE

RESERVED FOR FINANCIAL INSTITUTION USE*

*FEDERAL RESERVE BOARD OF GOVERNORS REG. CC

Tyra M. Burns **107**
4500 Red Maple Lane, Apt. 115
Maplewood, OH 44920

DATE ______________ 98-765/43

PAY TO THE
ORDER OF ______________ $ ______

______________ **DOLLARS**

FCB First City Bank

MEMO ______________ ______________

⑆98765⑆ 12⑈345678⑈ FOR CLASSROOM USE ONLY

ENDORSE HERE

DO NOT WRITE, STAMP OR SIGN BELOW THIS LINE

RESERVED FOR FINANCIAL INSTITUTION USE*

*FEDERAL RESERVE BOARD OF GOVERNORS REG. CC

Tyra M. Burns **108**

4500 Red Maple Lane, Apt. 115

Maplewood, OH 44920

DATE ____________ 98-765/43

PAY TO THE ORDER OF ____________ $ ______

____________ **DOLLARS**

FCB First City Bank

MEMO ____________

⑆98765⑆ 12⑉345678⑈

FOR CLASSROOM USE ONLY

ENDORSE HERE

DO NOT WRITE, STAMP OR SIGN BELOW THIS LINE

RESERVED FOR FINANCIAL INSTITUTION USE*

*FEDERAL RESERVE BOARD OF GOVERNORS REG. CC

Tyra M. Burns **106**

4500 Red Maple Lane, Apt. 115

Maplewood, OH 44920

DATE ____________________ 98-765/43

PAY TO THE ORDER OF ____________________ $ ________

____________________ DOLLARS

FCB First City Bank

MEMO ____________________ ____________________

⑆98765⑆ 12⑈345678⑈ FOR CLASSROOM USE ONLY

ENDORSE HERE

DO NOT WRITE, STAMP OR SIGN BELOW THIS LINE

RESERVED FOR FINANCIAL INSTITUTION USE*

*FEDERAL RESERVE BOARD OF GOVERNORS REG. CC

Tyra M. Burns **105**

4500 Red Maple Lane, Apt. 115

Maplewood, OH 44920

DATE ______________________ 98-765/43

PAY TO THE ORDER OF ______________________ $ ________

______________________ **DOLLARS**

First City Bank

MEMO ______________________

⑆98765⑆ 12⑈345678⑈

FOR CLASSROOM USE ONLY

ENDORSE HERE

DO NOT WRITE, STAMP OR SIGN BELOW THIS LINE

RESERVED FOR FINANCIAL INSTITUTION USE*

*FEDERAL RESERVE BOARD OF GOVERNORS REG. CC

Tyra M. Burns **104**

4500 Red Maple Lane, Apt. 115

Maplewood, OH 44920

DATE ________________ 98-765/43

PAY TO THE
ORDER OF ______________________ $ ________

________________________________ **DOLLARS**

FCB First City Bank

MEMO ________________ ________________

⑆987654⑆ 12⑈345678⑈

FOR CLASSROOM USE ONLY

ENDORSE HERE

DO NOT WRITE, STAMP OR SIGN BELOW THIS LINE

RESERVED FOR FINANCIAL INSTITUTION USE*

*FEDERAL RESERVE BOARD OF GOVERNORS REG. CC

Tyra M. Burns **103**
4500 Red Maple Lane, Apt. 115
Maplewood, OH 44920

DATE ____________________ 98-765/43

PAY TO THE
ORDER OF ______________________________ $ __________

____ **DOLLARS**

FCB **First City Bank**

MEMO ____________________ ____________________

⑆987654⑆ 12⑈345678⑈

FOR CLASSROOM USE ONLY

ENDORSE HERE

DO NOT WRITE, STAMP OR SIGN BELOW THIS LINE

RESERVED FOR FINANCIAL INSTITUTION USE*

*FEDERAL RESERVE BOARD OF GOVERNORS REG. CC

Tyra M. Burns
4500 Red Maple Lane, Apt. 115
Maplewood, OH 44920

102

DATE ______________________ 98-765/43

PAY TO THE
ORDER OF ______________________________ $ __________

____ **DOLLARS**

FCB First City Bank

MEMO ______________________ ______________________

⑆98765⑆ 12⑈345678⑈

FOR CLASSROOM USE ONLY

ENDORSE HERE

DO NOT WRITE, STAMP OR SIGN BELOW THIS LINE

RESERVED FOR FINANCIAL INSTITUTION USE*

*FEDERAL RESERVE BOARD OF GOVERNORS REG. CC

Tyra M. Burns **101**
4500 Red Maple Lane, Apt. 115
Maplewood, OH 44920

DATE ______________ 98-765/43

PAY TO THE
ORDER OF ______________ $ ______

______________ **DOLLARS**

FCB First City Bank

MEMO ______________ ______________

⑆987651⑆ 12⑈345678⑈ FOR CLASSROOM USE ONLY

CHECK NUMBER	DATE	DESCRIPTION OF TRANSACTION	PAYMENT/ DEBIT (−)		FEE (−)	✓	DEPOSIT/ CREDIT (+)		BALANCE FWD $	
			$				$			

CHECK NUMBER	DATE	DESCRIPTION OF TRANSACTION	PAYMENT/ DEBIT (−)		FEE (−)	✓	DEPOSIT/ CREDIT (+)		BALANCE FWD	
									$	
			$				$			

CHECK NUMBER	DATE	DESCRIPTION OF TRANSACTION	PAYMENT/ DEBIT (−)		FEE (−)	✓	DEPOSIT/ CREDIT (+)		BALANCE FWD	
									$	
			$				$			

CHECK NUMBER	DATE	DESCRIPTION OF TRANSACTION	PAYMENT/ DEBIT (−)		FEE (−)	✓	DEPOSIT/ CREDIT (+)		BALANCE FWD	
									$	
			$				$			

CHECK NUMBER	DATE	DESCRIPTION OF TRANSACTION	PAYMENT/ DEBIT (−)		FEE (−)	✓	DEPOSIT/ CREDIT (+)		BALANCE FWD	
									$	
			$				$			

CHECK NUMBER	DATE	DESCRIPTION OF TRANSACTION	PAYMENT/ DEBIT (−)		FEE (−)	✓	DEPOSIT/ CREDIT (+)		BALANCE FWD	
									$	
			$				$			

CHECK NUMBER	DATE	DESCRIPTION OF TRANSACTION	PAYMENT/ DEBIT (−)		FEE (−)	✓	DEPOSIT/ CREDIT (+)		BALANCE FWD	
									$	
			$				$			

CHECK NUMBER	DATE	DESCRIPTION OF TRANSACTION	PAYMENT/ DEBIT (−)		FEE (−)	✓	DEPOSIT/ CREDIT (+)		BALANCE FWD	
									$	
			$				$			

CHECK NUMBER	DATE	DESCRIPTION OF TRANSACTION	PAYMENT/ DEBIT (−)		FEE (−)	✓	DEPOSIT/ CREDIT (+)		BALANCE FWD	
									$	
			$				$			

CHECK NUMBER	DATE	DESCRIPTION OF TRANSACTION	PAYMENT/ DEBIT (−)		FEE (−)	✓	DEPOSIT/ CREDIT (+)		BALANCE FWD	
									$	
			$				$			

CHECK NUMBER	DATE	DESCRIPTION OF TRANSACTION	PAYMENT/ DEBIT (−)		FEE (−)	✓	DEPOSIT/ CREDIT (+)		BALANCE FWD	
									$	
			$				$			

CHECK NUMBER	DATE	DESCRIPTION OF TRANSACTION	PAYMENT/ DEBIT (–)		FEE (–)	✓	DEPOSIT/ CREDIT (+)		BALANCE FWD	
									$	
			$				$			

CHECK NUMBER	DATE	DESCRIPTION OF TRANSACTION	PAYMENT/ DEBIT (−)		FEE (−)	✓	DEPOSIT/ CREDIT (+)		BALANCE FWD	
									$	
			$				$			

CHECK NUMBER	DATE	DESCRIPTION OF TRANSACTION	PAYMENT/ DEBIT (−)		FEE (−)	✓	DEPOSIT/ CREDIT (+)		BALANCE FWD	
									$	
			$				$			

CHECK NUMBER	DATE	DESCRIPTION OF TRANSACTION	PAYMENT/ DEBIT (−)		FEE (−)	✓	DEPOSIT/ CREDIT (+)		BALANCE FWD	
									$	
			$				$			

CHECK NUMBER	DATE	DESCRIPTION OF TRANSACTION	PAYMENT/ DEBIT (−)		FEE (−)	✓	DEPOSIT/ CREDIT (+)		BALANCE FWD	
									$	
			$				$			

CHECK NUMBER	DATE	DESCRIPTION OF TRANSACTION	PAYMENT/ DEBIT (−)		FEE (−)	✓	DEPOSIT/ CREDIT (+)		BALANCE FWD	
									$	
			$				$			